Please remember that this is a library book,
and that it belongs only temporarily to each
person who uses it. Be considerate. Do
not write in this, or any, library book.

WITHDRAWN

ART LESSONS ON A SHOESTRING

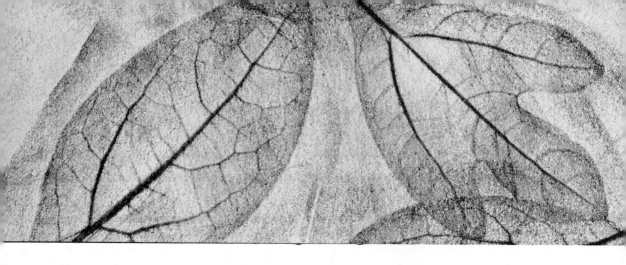

ART LESSONS ON A SHOESTRING

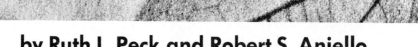

by Ruth L. Peck and Robert S. Aniello

Three-dimensional photographs
by Thomas Austin Cramer

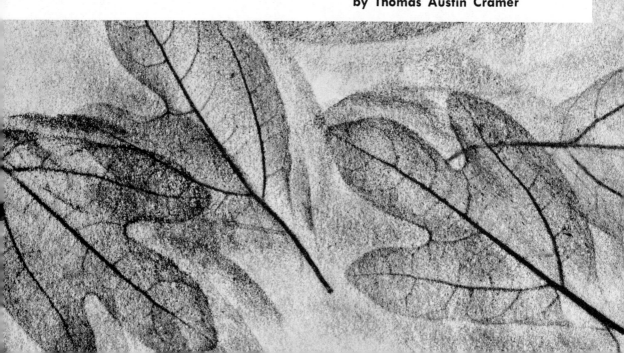

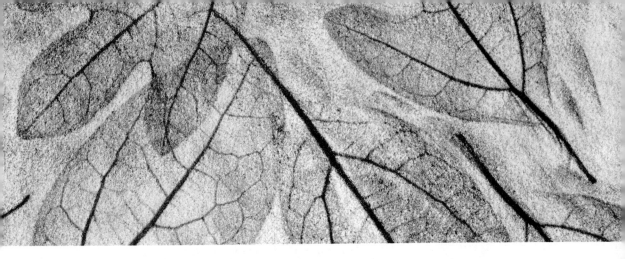

New Ideas for Practical
Art Lessons in the
Elementary School

PARKER PUBLISHING COMPANY, INC., WEST NYACK, N.Y.

Art Lessons on a Shoestring: New Ideas for
Practical Art Lessons in the Elementary School,
by Ruth L. Peck and Robert S. Aniello

© 1968, BY

PARKER PUBLISHING COMPANY, INC.

WEST NYACK, N. Y.

ALL RIGHTS RESERVED NO PART OF THIS BOOK
MAY BE REPRODUCED IN ANY FORM, BY MIMEO-
GRAPH OR ANY OTHER MEANS, WITHOUT PER-
MISSION IN WRITING FROM THE PUBLISHER.

LIBRARY OF CONGRESS
CATALOG CARD NUMBER 68-25940

PRINTED IN THE UNITED STATES OF AMERICA

B & P

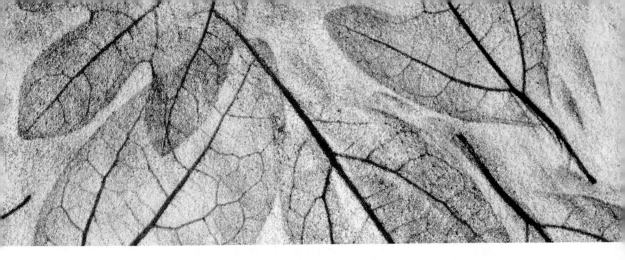

New Ideas for Practical
Art Lessons in the
Elementary School

PARKER PUBLISHING COMPANY, INC., WEST NYACK, N.Y.

Art Lessons on a Shoestring: New Ideas for Practical Art Lessons in the Elementary School, by Ruth L. Peck and Robert S. Aniello

© 1968, BY

PARKER PUBLISHING COMPANY, INC.

WEST NYACK, N. Y.

ALL RIGHTS RESERVED NO PART OF THIS BOOK MAY BE REPRODUCED IN ANY FORM, BY MIMEO-GRAPH OR ANY OTHER MEANS, WITHOUT PER-MISSION IN WRITING FROM THE PUBLISHER.

LIBRARY OF CONGRESS
CATALOG CARD NUMBER 68-25940

PRINTED IN THE UNITED STATES OF AMERICA

B & P

372.52
P367a

To the Teacher

IF YOU ARE LIKE MOST ELEMEN-
tary classroom teachers, you have many questions and doubts about teaching
art. You know that good art is creative art. But how in the world can you
be creative and, more important, how can you help the children in your
class to be creative? You need ideas—where do you look for them? You
have a dozen subjects to teach, and each one takes time to plan and prepare;
you just don't have the time to search for art ideas or to experiment on
your own. There are too many other things to do. You may even lack confidence in your ability to teach art.

But then you have another problem, too. You may hear about a wonderfully creative art lesson—but it takes materials you just don't have.
It would be fine, you say, if you had an abundance of materials. But your
supplies are limited—almost non-existent. You need ideas for art on a
shoestring!

It is likely you have one or more of these complaints—lack of ideas,
lack of time, and lack of materials. Most elementary classroom teachers do!
Perhaps, though, you are the exception. You have lots of ideas and an
abundance of art materials—but you are bored. You've used crayons in
all the usual ways, you've had some delightful painting lessons, you've used
clay and cloth and chalk and charcoal and all the other expensive materials
on the stockroom shelves. You're tired of all of them and you want to know
what else you can do. You want to be different.

So whatever your problem is—lack of time, lack of materials, lack of
ideas, lack of enthusiasm—you need help in planning creative and worthwhile art lessons. And it is for you that this book has been written. It has
been written to save you time; it has been written to give you creative art
lessons that can be presented in spite of a limited or almost non-existent
art budget; it has been written to add zest to lagging enthusiasm; it has
been written for you so that you may enjoy teaching art and so that you

v

32165

may make it both pleasant and worthwhile for your students. It has been written to give you confidence in yourself and in the lessons you teach.

Both of the authors are art teachers in elementary schools. They understand the problems you face and the possibilities you have. They have improvised with "found" art materials, sometimes from necessity and sometimes for the sheer fun of it.

They realize, too, that children are often more intrigued by simple, cast-off materials than they are by expensive, purchased supplies. They are reminded of the little child who spent a few minutes playing with a gleaming, new, expensive toy truck. Then he forgot it while he spent the rest of the day playing with the large packing box the toy had come in. He was being creative! The authors believe that the children in your classes will react much the same way. They may take regular art materials for granted, but they will be fascinated by what they can do with the odd assortment of materials they find in the backyard, the garage, the kitchen or other parts of the house.

So, no excuses! You can have creative art on a shoestring! You can have art lessons of value. You can enjoy them, too! The practical, easy-to-follow lessons in this book are in accord with the best of modern art education. They encourage the child to be different, to be creative. They make it possible for the child's art to be as personal as the individual who created it. They are presented on a pleasant person-to-person basis.

This book will help you select and plan art activities that will result in individual, creative expression that has value to every child. Regardless of how extensive or how limited your art supplies are, this book puts into your hands meaningful art lessons. It helps you consider the purposes of your lessons; it suggests simple ways to organize your lessons; it suggests ways to vary the lessons so that they may be used at different grade levels— or ways to vary the same lesson so that basic concepts will be retained by the children.

We sincerely hope that because of this book you and your classes will find art increasingly pleasant and profitable.

RUTH L. PECK
ROBERT S. ANIELLO

Contents

ART LESSONS ON A
SHOESTRING

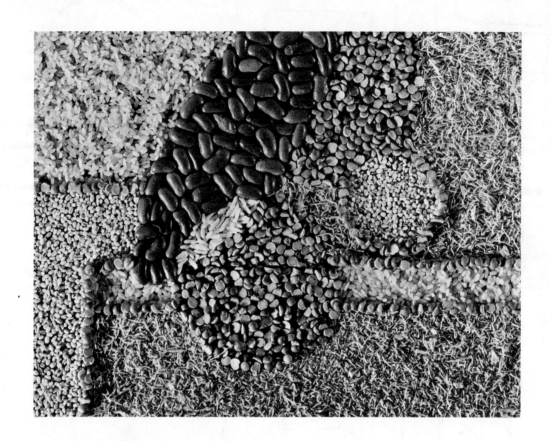

OBJECTIVES

1. To introduce collage as an art form.

2. To create texture and pattern in a non-objective picture.

3. To introduce the possibility of using "non-art" materials in a picture or composition.

(For Grades 1 through 6)

Lesson One:

LOOK BEYOND THE LABEL

Dried Foods Collage

LOOK BEYOND THE LABEL! LOOK INSIDE the box and try to forget how food looks when it's cooked, and you may find a whole new creative world. In looking for new ideas and media, we often neglect the obvious. Imagine the surprise and exictement of your students when you ask them to search the cupboards and pantry for any kind of dried foods. For an art lesson? Tell them to bring in cereals of all shapes, macaroni of all sizes, together with beans, peas, lentils—anything that's dry and firm.

Spread out the donations in piles on a table in front of the room so that each kind of food is visible and so that the class can see the differences in color, texture, size, and shape. Point out how the pile of cereal looks rough and jagged while the peas look smooth and round. Talk about the soft colors, how pleasing they are with no one color jumping out at you. Even on the table they lose their food quality and seem to be a large interesting design. That's our artistic problem—how to make a non-objective collage of these assorted materials.

Use chalk or light colored crayon to plan a smooth flowing design on a piece of cardboard—old shirt boards do just fine or pieces of cardboard boxes from the stockroom can be used. Talk about lines, how they can be soft and gentle or sharp and exciting. Start with a large freeform shape very much like a tear drop or an amoeba and then finish the space with more lines. Lines may cross to form smaller shapes, but caution the class not to make shapes too small or too numerous.

Have each child select a small handful of one type of food to start. Spread the surface of one shape with glue and quickly pour on the dried foods, pressing down slightly. Make sure that every space is filled, and gently shake off the extra foods. Continue until the entire design is covered. Caution the students to plan the different areas ahead of time so that no two adjoining spaces are filled with the same materials. The food may also be placed on the glued surface one piece at a time, very much like a mosaic. This process, of course, takes longer but may be more satisfying to the student.

The overall effect is one of simple beauty and elegance which will enhance any room or bulletin board. You'll be very proud and pleased when visitors marvel at your cleverness. The soft beauty of the colors and the flowing lines will add a quiet charm to your room. This all can be yours if you look beyond the label.

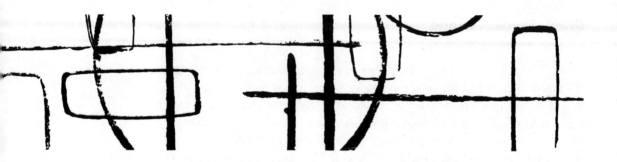

Make It Easy—for Yourself!

1. Avoid the use of pencils to form the design as the resulting shapes tend to be tight and small.
2. Be sure to have dried foods of many textures and colors.
3. Use low containers such as paper plates to display the food-stuffs.
4. Have some kind of small container such as a paper cup for each child. These may be used to transport the foods from the supply area to the desk. Extra supplies may be returned to the table and another kind taken back to the desk.
5. Make sure the desks are covered with newspaper to protect their surfaces from the glue.
6. Shake the excess unglued foods from the design onto the news-paper, and put it back into the cup to be returned to the supply area.

Variations

1. Use dried foods for only part of the design, filling in some spaces with construction paper or magazine pages or newspaper.
2. Cover the entire surface with one dried food and then paint a design or picture over it.

3. Paint or crayon a non-objective design. Outline the shapes with the glue and sprinkle on crushed cereals. Crush the cereal (cornflake type) in your hands until it is almost a powder.

4. On a solid color background, make a linear or scribble design with the glue and sprinkle on the crushed cereal, or place solid foods like beans or peas, one at a time, creating a textured line design.

5. Plan a realistic picture with crayon on a sheet of heavy paper or cardboard. Keep the plan simple and uncluttered. Fill in one area at a time with glue, and add the dried foods until the entire picture is covered. Plan ahead so that two of the same type of food will not come next to one another.

6. Cover the cardboard with colored paper or paint, then plan a realistic picture. Draw one large object such as a fish, bird, or butterfly. Cover the drawing with the different foods so that the object is a variety of colors and textures, making a subtle mosaic-like picture.

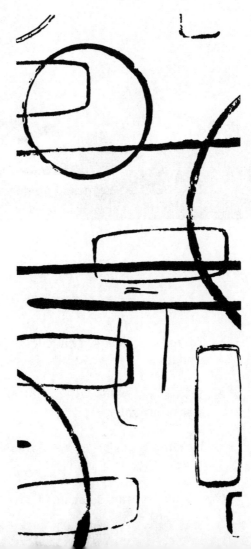

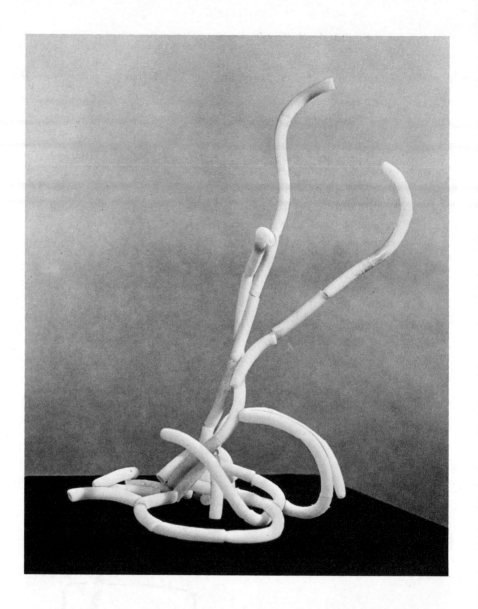

OBJECTIVES

1. To use a readily available material to introduce sculpture.

2. To use a novelty material to create a three-dimensional design.

3. To offer a choice of size, shape, and texture for a construction.

(For Grades 5 and 6; adapted to Grades 1 through 4)

Lesson Two:

BUON APPETITO

3-D Macaroni Sculpture

YOU CAN NOW HAVE INTERESTING pieces of sculpture, with an Italian flavor, adorning your classroom for a visual "Buon Appetito."

Constructions made from sticks, wire, cardboard, toothpicks, straws, and other materials are quite common now in the art world. Have you ever seen a construction made of macaroni? Why not? Think of the tremendous variety of shapes you can find in this ever popular food product. You can have shells; twists; wheels; sticks that are round, flat, skinny, or fat; and even tiny pastina. See the possibilities?

Freedom of choice in selection and building is paramount for good sculpture. Discuss what 3-D means, and that sculpture has now come to mean any three-dimensional construction created from a variety of materials. You can say that constructions are designs which stand up—they don't have to look like real things—just pure design.

Talk about the many different shapes of macaroni—the class may even introduce you to some new ones! Have the class start bringing in macaroni, a little at a time so that there is not too much of one kind. Stimulate young minds to think beyond tomato sauce!

To begin the sculpture start with three or four pieces of macaroni on a flat surface and attach them together with a fast drying glue. This will form the base of your construction upon which you will build your design. As the base dries, choose a few more pieces for the actual sculpture. These may be all one kind or all different kinds of macaroni. Slowly glue, place, and hold the pieces on the base until your design starts to grow. Remember to leave a lot of empty places, for we don't want a pyramid, but an interesting piece of sculpture that goes up and around and in and out. Height may be quickly formed with spaghetti or lasagne shafts. These can be used alone to make an interesting construction which is high, wide, and handsome.

The finished products may be sprayed, painted, or left alone. Display them around the room—and wish your visitors "buon appetito."

9

Make It Easy—for Yourself!

1. Make sure to have as many types of macaroni as possible.
2. Display each type of macaroni on a paper plate or in a pile.
3. Cover desks to prevent glue from damaging them.
4. Have children select only a few pieces at a time, coming back for more as needed.
5. Remind the class that macaroni is very fragile and must be treated with care.
6. Do not move or touch the finished constructions until they are dry.

Variations

1. Build a simple structure, then add colored paper, tissue paper, or cellophane in the open spaces. Use model-type cement to glue the cellophane.
2. Make a flat construction of spaghetti in geometric shapes, filling in the opening with more spaghetti to get a striped, criss-cross or plaid pattern. Tie thread or string on one of the outside edges and suspend as a mobile.

Variation for Lower Grades

Take a small piece of non-hardening clay, "play dough," or a flour and water dough and use this as a base to insert pieces of spaghetti or long macaroni of different lengths. This basic "tree" can be used for a variety of purposes. For example, in the spring you may want to paste on cut paper flowers for an indoor garden. At Easter it can become an Easter egg tree by pasting brightly decorated paper eggs on it. Fall leaves of red, yellow, and orange signify autumn. Simple freeform shapes make it "modern art."

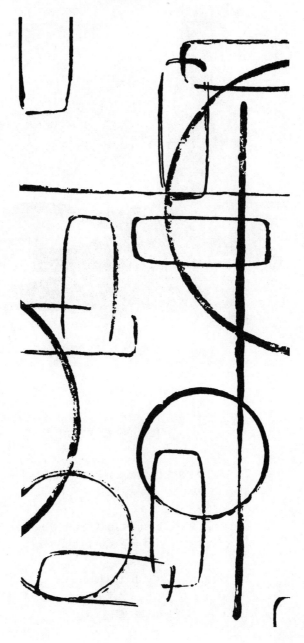

OBJECTIVES

1. To use a familiar household material in a new and exciting way.

2. To use both transparent and non-transparent materials together in the same picture.

3. To organize several objects into a single picture.

(For Grades K through 6)

Lesson Three:

PICTURE SANDWICHES

Wax Paper Transparencies

PERHAPS YOU THINK WAX PAPER is just for wrapping sandwiches. Well, it isn't. We're going to use it for *making* the sandwiches—picture sandwiches! And we'll be able to see through them, too!

Now how in the world can you make a picture sandwich? Why, that's easy. The wax paper will be the top and bottom parts that hold a filling together. So all you really have to do is decide what kind of a filling you would like—what kind of a picture sandwich you want it to be.

Think about what kind of a picture you would like to make. Perhaps it will be a landscape with trees and houses and people and anything you might see when you look around your neighborhood. Yes, it could be a sea picture—perhaps a tall, graceful sailboat in the water. Or you might make it an underwater scene with fat, round fish and long, slender ones. There might even be a strange octopus in it. Seaweed would belong in that kind of picture, too, wouldn't it?

Let's begin by folding a piece of wax paper in half. Then unfold it so that you have the top and bottom of a picture sandwich. Now I'll take a piece of colored construction paper and cut out the parts of my picture—the filling part of the sandwich. I'll cut out and arrange all the people or fish or houses or boats or whatever my sandwich is going to have in it. Oh, I'll leave some plain space—some wax paper, that is—around all the edges of my picture. That will keep anything from falling out later on. And of course I'll arrange my filling on only one half of the wax paper. The other half will cover the filling.

There—all the parts of my picture are in the filling, but there is one more thing I think it needs to be a good picture sandwich. It needs more color. So I'll just shave off some bits of an old crayon and add those to my picture. In your picture you might want it to be part of the sky or even the water.

With an open pair of scissors scrape off bits of crayon and let them drop on the wax paper part of your picture. Add more than one color if you want to.

13

When all the parts of the picture are in their right places, cover the filling with the other half of the wax paper—the top of the sandwich. Would the sandwich stay together if we left it this way? Certainly not! So we'll have to do something to make it stick together. We'll iron it! A funny thing to do to a sandwich, isn't it!

Slide a piece of cardboard or heavy paper under the wax paper sandwich. This will make a tray so that you can easily carry it to an ironing area which has been previously prepared. Lay cardboard and sandwich on the ironing area, and then carefully slide out the cardboard. Cover the sandwich with a piece of newspaper, and press it with a medium hot iron.

Why do you suppose we iron our sandwiches? That's right! The wax in the paper and in the crayons will melt and fasten the whole thing together. Then the filling won't be able to fall out.

When you remove the newspaper and hold the finished picture up to the window, there will be expressions of surprise and delight. Everyone will be eager to go to work on his own picture sandwich.

Give each child a piece of wax paper and have him fold it in half immediately. Then have him open it up so that he can arrange his filling on one of the inside halves. Arrange several colors of construction paper in an area where the children may choose what they need. Have a box of old crayons of assorted colors for the crayon shavings. A pair of scissors for each person and some cardboard for trays will be all the materials necessary. Urge the children to be original—to be different.

When the children finish their fillings, let them take turns bringing them to the ironing area (on cardboard trays), and pressing them with a medium hot iron. As the pictures are finished have each child hold his up to the window so the other children can see it. Then plan a more permanent display—pictures taped to the windows so they can be enjoyed for a longer time.

Make It Easy—for Yourself!

1. Tear the wax paper into pieces about two feet long and fold in half into an approximate square. Or tear the wax paper into slightly shorter pieces and fold them in half for a long, vertical picture. For a kindergarten class you may want to have the paper folded in half before you give it to the children.
2. You may have a cardboard (or heavy paper) for each child—or a group of children may take turns sharing one piece.
3. Be sure the children arrange their "fillings" on only half of the wax paper—so the other half may be folded over it.

4. Leave a wax paper edge around the whole picture. Otherwise the wax would not seal and the parts of the picture could fall out.
5. Prepare an ironing area by having a thick pile of newspaper— to prevent the heat from penetrating to the surface of the table or desk.
6. Have several extra pieces of newspaper at the ironing area so that a fresh piece will be available when needed to place on the pictures before ironing.
7. Have the children print their names on small pieces of paper and insert them near the bottom of their pictures. This can be ironed into the picture for easy identification.
8. Supervise the ironing area to be certain the iron is used correctly.
9. Have masking tape (or other adhesive) available so that finished pictures may be immediately displayed at the windows— or display them on a white paper on a bulletin board.

Variations

1. Use natural materials that have been dried and pressed (leaves, ferns, grasses) between pieces of wax paper. Bits of wax crayon may be added to give extra color.
2. Use other kinds of paper in place of the construction paper: gift wrapping, tissue, newspaper, magazines.

Variation for Upper Grades

Make a three-dimensional picture. Draw a simple object on a piece of 12″ x 18″ paper. Avoid details and keep all areas large. Place a piece of wax paper over the drawing and trace the drawing by pressing heavily on the wax paper with a pencil. Place bits of colored paper within the drawn shape. Bits of old crayons may be shaved into the shape also to add color and body. Place another piece of wax paper over the whole thing and press with a warm iron. Be sure the edges around the drawing are sealed. Cut along the traced line on the wax paper (it will still show). Punch a hole in the top of the finished transparency so that it may be suspended as a mobile.

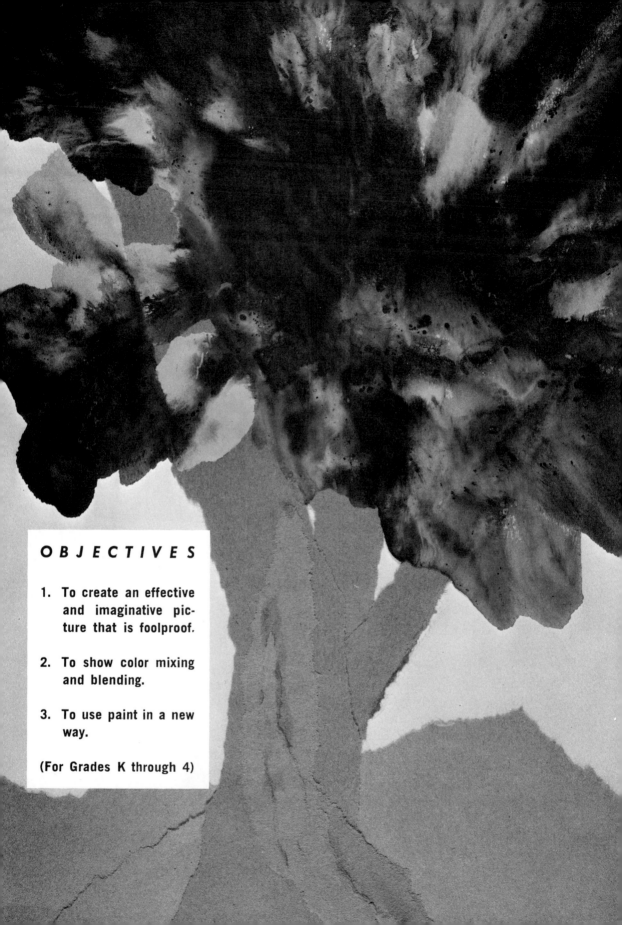

OBJECTIVES

1. To create an effective and imaginative picture that is foolproof.

2. To show color mixing and blending.

3. To use paint in a new way.

(For Grades K through 4)

Lesson Four:

THE BLOB

Autumn Trees with Paint

THIS IS NOT A SCIENCE FICTION
story, although the experimental and exploratory methods make it interesting. The blob is easy to make and has many uses and effects. All you need is paint of various colors and wax paper found in any kitchen.

For very young children, let's make some fall trees. Take a piece of 12″ x 18″ paper—white, light blue, light green, or any other light color as a background. Talk about trees, how they are made up of a trunk, branches, and leaves. Ask the class if anyone ever touched a tree trunk. How did it feel? Was it smooth or rough? When you've decided that a tree's bark is rough, ask how we can show rough or bumpy edges with a piece of brown or black 9″ x 12″ construction paper. This edge can be achieved by tearing! We can tear out a strip the entire length of the 9″ x 12″ construction paper for the trunk and smaller strips for branches. Each child can develop his own tree—short and fat, tall and thin, very straight, or gnarled and dwarfed. When the tree is put together and pasted down on the larger paper, we're ready for our foliage.

Each child should now have a piece of wax paper the same size (12″ x 18″) as the background. Choose the paint for your trees to fit the season. In this case choose red, orange, and yellow to suggest autumn colors. Have the paint in containers from which a small amount of paint can be poured. On each picture pour a small blob of each color just above the trunk of the tree. The colors can be placed next to each other or one above the other. The child now places the wax paper over the paint and spreads the colors out and up towards the edges of the paper. The colors mix and create beautiful patterns and mixtures which look very much like clusters of leaves. By using wax paper, the colors can be seen and therefore controlled.

Keep the wax paper on over night. Then when the paint has dried, peel it off. Some of the wax will remain on the paint, giving it a soft sheen. Everyone will be delighted and proud of the handsome tree he has created from a beautiful blob.

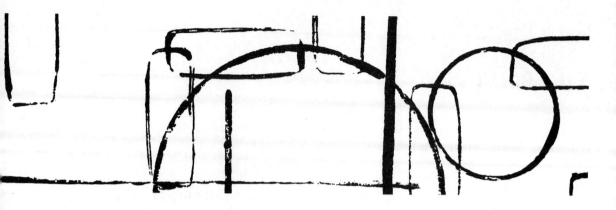

Make It Easy—for Yourself!

1. If making a tall tree use the paper vertically.
2. Paper cups or detergent bottles may be used as paint containers from which the paint is poured.
3. Make sure the paint is absolutely dry before removing the wax paper—to avoid tearing and sticking.
4. Cover desks with newspaper in case paint is pushed beyond the edges of the wax paper.
5. Do not overwork the wax paper, for it becomes wet and tears easily.

Variations

1. Cut out a vase from a folded piece of 9″ x 12″ paper. Open it and paste it near the bottom of a 12″ x 18″ piece of construction paper (light green, light blue, or white). Pour out red, yellow, blue, and white (or any combination) of paint just above the vase. Apply the wax paper and spread the paint for a beautiful bouquet of flowers.
2. Cut out individual stems and leaves from green construction paper and paste them down in a pleasing grouping on a 12″ x 18″ light color paper. Talk about the slender and graceful lines of stems and the variety of leaves. Stress the importance of making the picture fit the paper. At the top of each stem pour out a small amount of paint. Use at least two colors. Each child now can create individual blossoms of his own design by moving the paint under the wax paper.

Variations for Higher Grades

1. The trees and flowers techniques may be used as part of a picture in order to make it more interesting. Pictures made from cut paper, paint, chalk, or charcoal can be enhanced by the blob.
2. The blob can be used most effectively as a forest background for a large mural done in any medium.

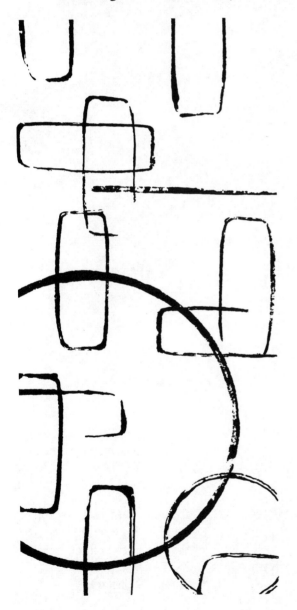

OBJECTIVES

1. To continue to learn about the blending of colors.

2. To introduce a simple form of printing.

3. To insure an art lesson which will guarantee success for every child.

(For Grades K through 4)

Lesson Five:

BLOB PRINTS

Mixing Colors for Prints

THE BLOB CAN GROW AND GROW and grow in both size and ideas. We have seen how the blob can be used effectively to make realistic pictures. Now let's see how it can be used in a multitude of projects in which exciting use of color is desired.

Let's pull some blob prints. Create your blob of mixed colors by pouring out small amounts of paint on a background paper. This background can be anything from construction paper to brown wrapping paper. Make sure it is fairly strong, so avoid a lightweight paper such as newsprint. Oak tag is most desirable because of its lack of porosity. Place a piece of wax paper on top of the paint puddles and spread them until they mix and form new colors and exciting patterns and shapes. Use at least two contrasting colors. The primary colors (red, yellow, and blue) plus white are best because you can achieve the secondary colors plus pastels with them.

When the blob is formed to your satisfaction and before the wax paper gets too wet, pull off the wax paper. The design left on the wax paper is in itself a print which can be allowed to dry and then can be framed with paper for a transparent non-objective design. When placed in a window, these designs take on a brilliant depth of color, interesting patterns, and unusual textures.

After the wax paper has been removed, other prints may be taken from the blob on the background paper by putting another colored or white paper over it. Rub the overlaying paper gently, then pull it off for another print. This can be repeated for as long as the blob will last.

These non-objective designs can stand alone or can be adapted for many other exciting pictures. This blob technique can be used to teach color, showing how the primary colors can produce the secondary colors. It also can show the warm effect of red, yellow, and orange—or the coolness of blue, green, and purple. It can teach how to achieve pastels by using colors and white.

Learning about color is fun for the class and painless for the teacher when you let the blob take over.

Make It Easy—for Yourself!

1. Paper cups or detergent bottles may be used as paint containers from which the paint can be poured.
2. Remove the wax paper as soon as the design is formed and while paint is wet.
3. Cover desks with newspaper to catch any paint.
4. Do not overwork the paints or they may become muddy and dry.
5. Prepare a drying area covered with newspapers on which to place the wet prints.
6. Plan to teach only one color lesson at a time, for example: warm colors only, or blending primary colors to create the secondary colors—but not both at the same time.

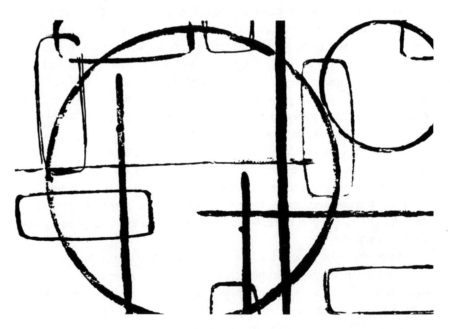

Variations

1. Use your dried prints to cut out colorful flowers, birds, leaves, insects, or anything else your imagination dictates. Mount them on a dark background for beautifully realistic pictures.
2. Find a realistic picture within your blob print. Then outline it with black paint, crayon, or dark magic markers.

3. Cut out a black silhouette picture and paste it down on the dried blob which will make an exciting background for it. Black paint or markers may be used instead of black paper.

4. Cut an object out of the center of a piece of construction paper and put this frame over the dried paint. Your object now becomes one of many colors.

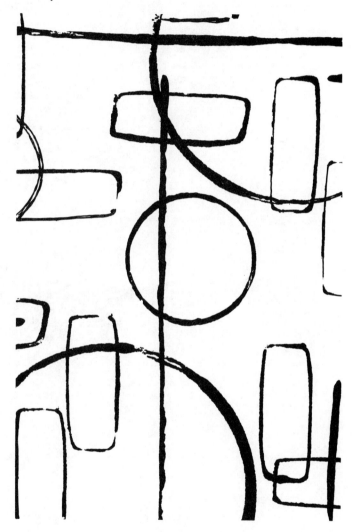

OBJECTIVES

1. To introduce sculpture to children.

2. To stimulate an awareness of three-dimensional art.

3 To create simple and satisfying classroom sculpture.

(For Grades 4 through 6)

Lesson Six:

FOILED AGAIN!

Aluminum Foil Sculpture

No need to cry "FOILED AGAIN" when trying to teach sculpture in the classroom. If you look in your kitchen you can find a fascinating material which will answer your creative needs. It's lightweight, shiny, pliable, durable, fun to touch, and it can be crumpled, torn, cut, bent, rolled, and twisted. Of course you know what it is— aluminum foil. You've probably used it for cooking because it is so easy to line pans with. Take this molding quality a step farther and you can create beautiful sculptures right in your classroom.

Because it is so wonderful to work with, aluminum foil can be handled in many different ways. Marvelous abstract constructions can be made simply by tearing, rolling, and twisting pieces of foil together so that the finished result looks like a metal sculpture. This lesson is particularly effective if large quantities of foil are at hand.

If more realistic sculptures are desired, and the amount of foil is limited, use newspaper or newsprint or old tissue paper as a base. Supply the class with common pins and you have all the necessities for exciting sculptures.

Starting with the newspaper, crumple it or roll it into the approximate shape of the object being made. This should be just a general form with no protrusions or details. Round forms may turn into heads, ovals may be the beginning of a fish or bird, a large roll may be the body of a reptile, snake, or butterfly. Cover the entire shape with foil and pin it to hold it in position. Details may be formed with only foil pinned to the basic form, or if large or stronger units are needed, foil-covered paper may be pinned into position. Now your basic oval becomes a fish when a tail, fins, eyes, and scales are molded and pinned onto it. Your sphere becomes a bust when a foil covered neck is attached, a nose molded from foil is pinned on, and eyes and mouth are added. Pinning is the easiest way to fasten foil parts together, but glue or cement may also be used.

When colored foil is available (perhaps from around a flower pot), there is no problem in adding details because the colors contrast and stand

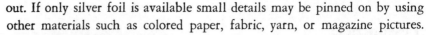

out. If only silver foil is available small details may be pinned on by using other materials such as colored paper, fabric, yarn, or magazine pictures.

Foil is a marvel to use in the classroom because it is so supple and so appealing to everyone. Imaginations can run wild as three-dimensional objects appear from the fingers of young people. You'll be surprised and happy to see all the wonderful creatures who will greet you every day from their honored positions of display around the room, and what's most important when it comes to sculpture, you'll never be—foiled again!

Make It Easy—for Yourself!

1. Try to show the class examples of contemporary sculptures made from different materials such as metal, wood, wire, sticks, and junk. This will help them to understand that sculpture is more than a statue in the park.
2. Have a good supply of pins available but pass out only a few at a time.
3. Have the class suggest simple forms which may become realistic objects.
4. If foil is not available from school supplies, have the children bring it in prior to the day of the lesson to make sure there is enough. Used but clean foil is suitable for sculpture.
5. Whenever possible, double layers of foil should be used for greater strength, especially when adding small appendages.
6. Fold under all edges for a stronger shape and cleaner appearance.

Variation

Try making a bas-relief sculpture on a background. Start with a base of construction paper and glue pieces of an object or picture down so that only a part of the foil is attached to the background. For example, if you wanted to make a large blossom, shape the petals out of foil and glue only the ends of them around a center. The rest of the petals can be molded up and out for a three-dimensional flower.

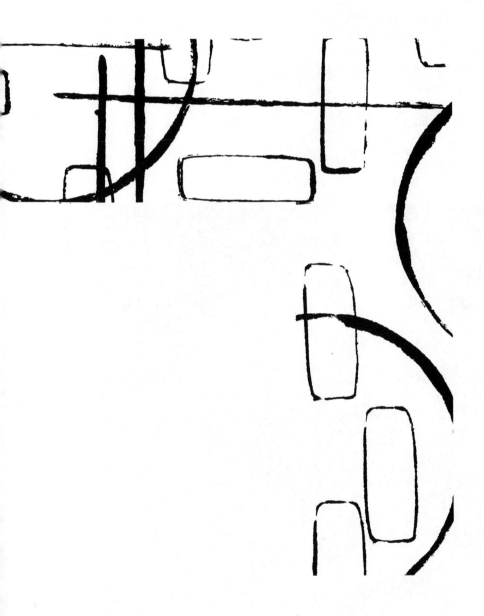

OBJECTIVES

1. To create a two-dimensional picture in an unusual medium.

2. To emphasize the use of line in drawing.

3. To create texture and pattern through line.

(For Grades 5 and 6)

Lesson Seven:

CARNIVAL MIDWAY

Foil Etching

YOU CAN BRING THE GAIETY AND CHARM OF A carnival midway to the classroom with an easy to do, clean, and effective lesson. You've seen artists at carnivals and fairs hammering out likenesses in copper. Well, you can get the same effect with ordinary aluminum foil and a dull pencil or ball point pen.

Don't let the simplicity of the lesson mislead you. There's a world of excitement in store when you see the results. All you need is a piece of foil—the size depends on how large you want the pictures to be—and a wad of newspapers. Each student should have an unwrinkled sheet of foil plus a whole folded newspaper on his desk. Great care must be taken to treat the foil gently and carefully so it won't wrinkle. Every wrinkle will interfere with the finished picture.

With a dull pencil or ball point pen, a picture is drawn on foil over the newspaper. Enough pressure must be given to create a raised surface on the opposite side of the foil. Too much pressure, however, will cause the foil to tear.

When the outlines of the picture (or design) are finished, solid areas may be indicated by making patterns with line. You may crisscross lines, put lines close together in straight or curved stripes, or you may make polka dots. Any series of marks in an area will give the feeling of solidity. Turn the foil over and you will find a picture of raised lines that gleams as if it were a metal plate. It is a good idea to staple the pictures on paper or cardboard for easier handling and to safeguard the delicacy of the drawing.

When put into simple paper frames, these etchings will add the sparkle and fun of a carnival midway to your room.

29

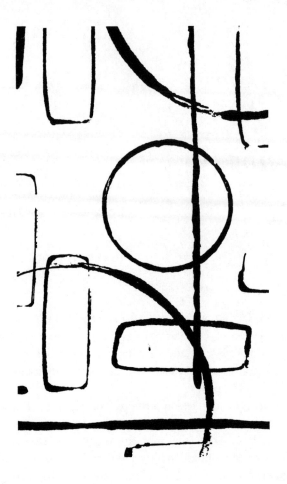

Make It Easy—for Yourself!

1. Make sure you have a thick wad of newspaper under the foil for a cushion. This will permit a deeper line in the foil.
2. Emphasize the danger of too much pressure which will cause the foil to tear.
3. To avoid wrinkles cut the foil with scissors instead of tearing it off the box.
4. Precut foil for easier distribution.
5. Gold or other colored foil may be used if it is available.
6. Avoid lettering because the image will be reversed.
7. Don't stack finished pictures as the pressure may flatten the design.
8. Staple or glue etchings to sturdy paper or cardboard which may be larger than the etching to form a frame.

Variation

Have the students draw one large object which would have pattern and texture on it—such as a fish with scales, a bird with feathers, or a butterfly with freeform designs on its wings. Carefully cut out the drawing and mount it (staple or cement) on a dark background.

OBJECTIVES

1. To realize the possibilities for creating art with ordinary materials found around the house.

2. To introduce a simple printing technique.

3. To develop a sense of rhythm through repetition.

(For Grades 3 through 6, adapted to Grades K through 2)

Lesson Eight:

GETTING READY TO COOK?

Gadget Printing

YOU'LL NEED SUCH THINGS AS KNIVES, FORKS, cooky cutters, potato mashers, cans, bottle tops—all kinds of things you find around the kitchen. Does it sound as though we're getting ready to cook? No, we're not going to cook—just do some printing.

For our gadget printing we'll need lots of things, so look around the kitchen for all the odd shapes you can find. Be sure they have a part you can hold on to and a part you can print. For example, a bottle top is thick enough to take hold of easily while you print with the rim on the open end. A penny, which might be almost the same diameter, would be too shallow to hold and print. So look for things like tops from spray cans, plastic pint fruit baskets, thermos bottle tops, corks, round or rectangular box tops, paper towel cores, sponges, empty spice cans—anything you can find to print.

Now let's see what we can do with this strange assortment of things. We'll need a large paper to make our picture on, and of course we'll need some tempera paint. No, we're not going to dip our objects into the paint. That would be too messy—and it wouldn't do a good job. So we'll need some kind of applicator for the paint. Watercolor brushes work fine, and so do easel brushes or paste brushes.

Begin by letting each child have a 9″ x 12″ practice paper and a palette paper with one color of paint. Have each person apply a small amount of paint to the printing edge of his gadget, then press it against his paper and lift it again. Oh, no, don't move your gadget when it is on the paper. That would be painting—and we are printing. Printing is just pressing down and lifting up. Down—up, down—up. Now re-ink your gadget and try it again. See, there is the shape of your box, or your fork, or your cooky cutter, or whatever your gadget is. Print several times more. Turn your gadget in different directions, overlap the prints.

Then try several more gadgets just to see what prints of them look like. You may want more than one kind of print on your good picture, so try several now. Decide which ones you want to keep for later use and which colors you would like to use, too. You may use only one color if you like, or you may want to use three or four colors on your printed picture. Show the class the five or six colors they may choose from.

After everyone has had a chance to experiment with several gadgets, stop all work. Show a few of the practice papers. Point out the interesting arrangements, good technique, variety of printing possibilities. Note the poor qualities, too—so they won't be repeated on the final picture. Someone *painted* with a gadget here, didn't he? See, it doesn't look like a print at all because it moved on the paper. Printing is just down and up, down and up. Point out, too, the places where too much paint has been used. Spoils the shape of the object you printed with, doesn't it?

Get rid of the practice paper—throw it away if you like, or put it aside to keep. But get it off the desk. Also collect and throw away the palette papers. Now with only a piece of newspaper on the desk—and a gadget or two—you are ready to begin again. Have a choice of white and several colors of 12″ x 18″ construction paper. Let each child have his choice. Give each child another palette paper and the one color paint he needs for a beginning.

While everyone is working you will be busy, too. Give children more paint as it is needed—of the same or additional colors. Encourage them to fill their papers. Let the prints go right off the edge of the paper—it will look better that way. Oh, no, no! You never put a thing in the middle of your picture and in each corner. That would be uninteresting, wouldn't it? Make your design move throughout the paper. Are you remembering to overlap? Would another kind of gadget help your picture? Or do you need a new color?

Comment, question, suggest until each printing is a masterpiece! Then you will be ready to clean up so that everyone can admire the finished productions.

The clean-up is easy. Have someone walk about the room with a box so that each person can put his gadgets into it. Later they can be washed—ready for another time. At the same time you could walk around the room and collect the palette papers. Just lay them lightly one on top of another and once in a while drop the whole pile in the wastebasket. There shouldn't be enough paint on the palette papers to cause any trouble. Then each child can slide his newspaper out from under his picture and fold the newspaper. Let someone collect them.

There—lots of fun, a new learning experience, an easy clean-up, and a roomful of beautiful pictures!

Make It Easy—for Yourself!

1. Have a good supply of gadgets so that each child may have several if he wishes. You may find them in other parts of the house besides the kitchen.
2. Cover all work areas with newspaper.
3. Use very little paint on a gadget, as too much paint tends to blot.
4. Repaint the gadget each time or two.
5. A piece of 6″ x 9″ paper makes a satisfactory palette. Place a tiny bit of tempera paint on it.
6. A paste brush makes an excellent tool for applying paint to the gadget. If you don't have paste brushes, use watercolor or easel brushes. Or use swab sticks—or make an applicator by folding a piece of scrap paper several times and then bending it in the middle.
7. The first printing of a plastic or metal gadget is not always satisfactory. When it is repainted more paint will adhere to it and print better.
8. Two or three children who sit close to each other may share the same gadgets.

Variations

1. Use potatoes or carrots in place of gadgets. Cut them in half and print that way—or make simple cuts into the flat surface before printing.
2. Make a realistic picture by choosing gadgets to print various parts of a person, animal, landscape.

Variations for Lower Grades

1. Use only one simple object (tongue depressor, paper cup, core from toilet tissue) to print with. Make the pictures realistic or non-objective.
2. Cut cardboard into small rectangular pieces (about 2″ x 4″). Print the edge of the cardboard as a straight line or bend it before printing.

OBJECTIVES

1. To create a three-dimensional object from a common material.

2. To make a simple puppet suitable for children of all ages.

3. To promote verbal expression through an art project.

(For Grades K through 6)

Lesson Nine:

IT'S IN THE BAG

Paper Bag Puppets

You've heard about the wee people of Ireland, but did you know that you've got little characters in your kitchen? It's true, and these creatures can lead to fun and excitement—it's in the bag!

All you need is a small paper bag to make a delightful hand puppet. Make sure the bag is the kind that has a flat bottom which is folded flat when not in use. This is the same style found at most supermarkets. The flat bottom is going to be the face of our puppet. The rest of the bag will represent the body or neck. Keep the bag flat on the desk with the bottom side folded up. Using almost any medium, it is possible to make an expressive face. You can draw a pair of eyes, a nose, and a mouth with a crayon. You can paint the features in, or you can cut them out of colored paper or magazines. Many other embellishments can be made with other material. You can use fabrics, buttons, dress trimmings, yarn, or string to add interesting details such as hats or collars.

Try cutting out large ears and adding fringed paper hair for a funny clown. Cut out a mask and a big black round nose and you may end up with a raccoon. Cut out one large eye, add a pair of antennae and a fang-like grin—and you have created a Martian.

When your puppet is finished, insert your hand all the way into the bag, so the bottom opens up flat. Hold your arm in a horizontal position (rather than upright) and you can make your puppet move in all directions.

Another way to create fantastic puppets is to treat the flat bottom of the bag as the upper part of the face, down to and including the upper lip. That is, the rectangle would include the eyes, nose, and the upper lip. The bottom lip is made on the body of the bag. This leads to more dramatic effects, for when your hand is inserted in the bag, you can move the rectangle of the bag and make the puppet's mouth open and close. Long teeth can be pasted under the upper lip, or make a protruding tongue which will add a new and exciting dimension to the puppet.

Although these puppets are simple to make, they lend themselves to any age group. They can be done very simply by young children, or they can become very sophisticated and intricate in the upper grades. Let your imagination be your guide and you'll find your puppet is—in the bag.

Make It Easy—for Yourself!

1. Try to exaggerate the features so as to make the puppet dramatic.
2. Use bright colors and make all parts large and simple.
3. Try to have each child think of a character before he starts— so he has a goal to reach.
4. Have the class bring in scraps of novelty materials such as fabric, old jewelry, lace, and trimming.

Variations

1. Any type of bag can be stuffed and tied at the bottom with string or rubber bands. A dowel or ruler can then be inserted as a handle. The whole bag becomes a giant head and can be treated in many different ways. The face can be painted or made from cut paper. Hair, ears, hat, ribbons, bows, can be added, using a multitude of materials to build any kind of character.
2. Using the above method, tie two sticks together to form a cross. The vertical stick is to hold and the horizontal stick becomes the shoulders. Fabric or painted newspaper can be used to

make a costume. One layer glued to the front of the shoulders hides the stick. Two layers, front and back, hide the stick and your hand from both sides. The costumes can be as simple or ornate as you want them to be. These giant puppets can be visual expansions of other work in social studies and literature.

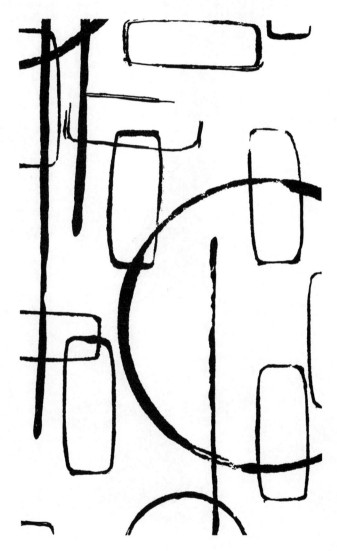

OBJECTIVES

1. To utilize a readily available material in an imaginative and creative way.

2. To create simple full-face masks for all ages and occasions.

3. To use the ancient art of mask-making to stimulate interest in other cultures and times.

(For Grades K through 3)

Lesson Ten:

DISAPPEARING ACT

Paper Bag Masks

TIRED OF THE SAME OLD FACES IN YOUR room? With one simple lesson you can transform your entire class into a scary menagerie of ghosts or ghouls or witch doctors—or monsters or Martians or anything else that can be thought up by young minds. The beauty of this lesson is that it can be done quite easily with simple and easy-to-get materials. All you need are willing subjects—and paper bags large enough to fit over their heads. You can be a magician and pull a fun-filled disappearing act.

The first step is to fit a bag over the head. Because a bag large enough to fit over a head will be too long, the bottom must be rolled up as for a collar effect, or cut off so that the bag will touch the top of the head when put on. The next fitting is to locate the eyes, nose, and mouth. This can be done easily enough by having the students use a crayon to mark the eyes, nose, and mouth while the bag is over their heads. Very young children may need help. Then the markings are cut out just big enough for clear vision and breathing.

Now that the preliminaries are over, the real fun and creativity begin. Have each child bring in any kind of junk from home—old jewelry, magazines, bits of string, yarn, or anything else that has color and texture. Make sure that each child has a character in mind before he begins, so that he has a goal to work toward. You can do characters for a play, or recreate masks of ancient civilizations, or make imaginary creatures from outer space, or anything else you may want to do.

Have each child flatten his bag on his work space with the cut out features up. The areas around the cut openings are now ready to be designed according to character. Large expressive eyes may be crayoned or painted or formed with cut colored paper around the openings. The same can be done for the mouth and nose. You can make fierce eyes and a mouth, or a three-dimensional nose, or a pair of "Twiggy" eyes with huge doll-like eyelashes and a pouting mouth. Witch doctors from Africa, or Kabuki masks from Japan, or even Mother Goose are only a few sources of inspiration for dramatic masks.

When the basic features have been put on, much embellishment can be added to create the desired effect. Yarn, string, colored strips of paper can become hair. Any lightweight "found" materials can be glued on to make dramatic eyebrows, crowns, ears, earrings, or anything the imagination dictates.

When all the masks are finished, one word from the magician—you, that is—and your whole class can disappear!

Make It Easy—for Yourself!

1. Have children bring from home materials they will need for their own puppets.
2. Have a few extra assorted materials which children may share. Display these on a table to stimulate imaginations.
3. Paste may be used for paper, but make sure you have glue available for heavier or non-porous materials.
4. Have an empty bulletin board available where puppets can be displayed after they have been modeled.

Variation

Cut down the bag so it will cover only the upper half of the face. These are suitable for more sophisticated harlequin-type masks.

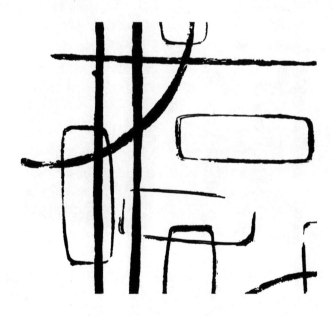

OBJECTIVES

1. To utilize a common material for an artistic purpose.

2. To create a useful and decorative item.

(For Grades K through 6)

Lesson Eleven:

THIS LITTLE KIDDIE
WENT TO MARKET

Shopping Bags

THE OLD NURSERY RHYME ABOUT THE THREE little piggies can take on a new and creative meaning by using a little poetic license. For our purposes, the first little kiddie went to market, proudly carrying a unique shopping bag decorated with his own hands, inspired by his own imagination.

Let's begin by discussing the possible uses for a shopping bag, besides the obvious one of toting things home from the store. It can be used for storage of personal items in your closet or classroom, or for packing to go on a trip, or to carry toys when on a visit, or for Mom's sewing or knitting supplies, or for many more reasons imaginative children can think of.

We can make a bag any size we want to by choosing the size paper bag that best suits our needs. We try to find an ordinary flat bottom paper bag which has no writing or store insignia on it. If this can't be done, don't worry, for we can use the writing to our own advantage.

If a plain, unadorned bag is used, we can use crayons to turn it into something special. It may be close to a holiday or the beginning of a new season, and this may be a clue as to how to decorate our bags. You may be studying a strange country or an ancient civilization. This, too, can lead to inspiration for motifs. Monograms, designed letters or numbers, country and city scenes, butterflies, birds, animals may also be considered for ideas for adornment. Try to determine the use of the bag and correlate the design with it. For example, the most obvious is a design of witches, goblins, ghosts, for a Halloween Trick-or-Treat bag.

If you want both sides of your bag to be alike, it is best to plan the picture for your bag on a plain piece of paper the same size as the bag. Complete the drawing with the actual colors to be used. This is the time for correcting mistakes and improving ideas. When this is finished, the back of the drawing can be covered with dark crayon, chalk, or pencil. Pin or tape the paper, picture side up, to the flattened paper bag. Go over the lines of the drawing with a pencil, bearing down firmly enough to transfer the back covering onto the bag. Take off the picture, correct any lines that did not come through, turn the bag over and repeat the entire process. Color in the picture on the bag, using a lot of crayon for a bright, sparkling picture.

Now it's time to attach a handle. Bright, heavy roving is ideal, but heavy twine or rope may also be used. If only yarn or light weight string is available, braid it for extra strength. Measure from the top of the bag down the side, around the bottom, and up the other side. Double this measurement and add enough extra twine for two loop handles. For a large grocery bag ten inches extra provides two five-inch handles. Tie the ends of the string together so that you now have a circle for roving or twine. Stretch out the circle to form an ellipse, placing the knot in the middle. The knot will eventually end up on the bottom of the bag in the center. Use a heavy duty glue to make two lines about four inches apart down the front center of the bag. Place the looped string on the glue with enough above the edge of the bag to form a handle. When this is secure, continue glueing and applying the string across the bottom and up the other side. You now have two loops extending above the edge of the bag forming two handles.

Think how happy, think how proud, think how lucky your class will feel as they proudly display their practical handiwork. Yes, this little kiddie is ready to go to market.

Make It Easy—for Yourself!

1. When attaching the handles make sure they are both even. This can be done by placing the knot in the center of the bottom of the bag.
2. Border the edge of the bag—right over the handles—with tape to strengthen both the handles and rim of the bag.
3. If possible, use a double bag, one inside the other, for greater durability.

Variations

1. If the bags have writing on them, cut paper can be used to create a design or picture. Often these emblems can be used as a guide for original and exciting motifs.

2. Use tempera paint to paint both sides of the bag in non-objective, flat designs for a contemporary look.

3. Use magazines to create exciting effects. Pictures of one subject—people, cars, houses—can be cut out and pasted on the bag as a montage. Or cut your own shapes from the many colors found in ads. Flowers, for example, can be very sophisticated if cut from clothing ads.

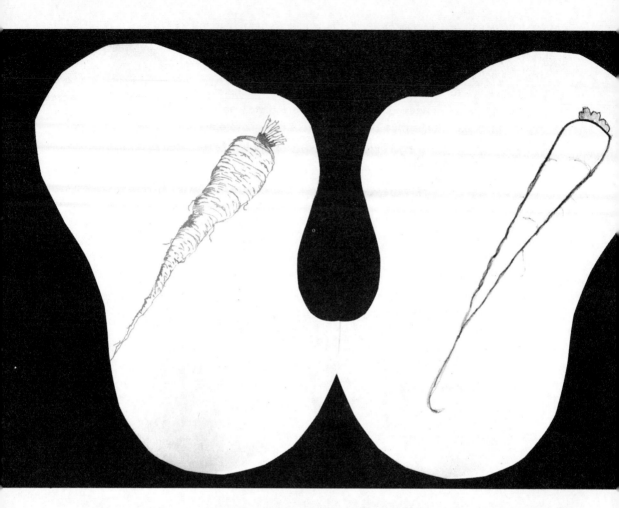

1. To stimulate the use of the "inner eye" for visual perception through the sense of touch.

2. To stress the use of touch as a tool to recognize and reproduce texture.

3. To train the eye and the hand to work together in drawing.

(For Grades 5 and 6; adapted to Grades 2 through 4)

Lesson Twelve:

BLIND MAN'S BUFF

Sensory Drawing

LET'S PLAY A GAME OF BLIND MAN'S BUFF! Can you imagine the response you'd get from your class if you used this as an introduction for an art lesson? If you remember the game, you'll recall how a blindfolded person seeks to identify other people by using his hands. This same principle can be used for an intriguing drawing lesson in which the artist uses his hands to study and identify and then reproduce an object.

The object of this artistic version of the classic game is to make young people aware of contour, texture, surface variations, and size. Many of us tend to look at things only superficially and this is why drawing seems too difficult to attempt. It is important for anyone who would like to draw better to become completely involved in his subject. This lesson is designed to increase that involvement by using the sense of touch to supplement the sense of sight.

In this version of the game a paper bag replaces the blindfold and ordinary and interesting objects replace the people. Have each of the children in the class bring in an object which they think has an interesting shape and/or texture. These objects can be anything—rocks, shells, coral, potatoes, ceramic ash trays, small pieces of driftwood, bark. Let each child have enough time to find something he likes and something he thinks will fool the class. Each object must be brought in a paper bag large enough for the object and someone's hand. The bag should have the donor's name on it to make sure he doesn't receive his own.

Since we are interested primarily in using touch to discover detail and texture, we can use pencils for this lesson. If possible, these pencils should be soft drawing pencils, but a good substitute can be found in the large pencils used by the primary grades. These are recommended because they tend to let the child use more freedom in drawing and help to avoid the danger of tight, dull drawings which ordinary pencils seem to stimulate. If these large pencils are not available, use crayons or charcoal, resorting to ordinary pencils only as a last measure.

As the paper bags arrive bearing their secret treasures, place them on

49

a table, counter, or the floor and let the class wonder and conjecture about what each bag contains. Try to impress upon the students that it is important that they don't tell what is in their bags. By the time the art period rolls around, the class should be eager and curious as to the contents of the bags.

Each child should have on his desk two pieces of drawing paper plus his drawing tool. One by one each person selects a bag and carries it to his seat—unopened! When everyone has a bag it is time to "see" what is in it—without looking. Each child must carefully open the bag, reach inside it, and without peeking try to determine the shape and texture of the object by feeling it. Suggest that each person close his eyes and try to see in his mind what the object looks like. After a few minutes of investigation, a life-size drawing of the object should be attempted. There should be more touching than drawing as the size of the piece is determined, then the texture, and any variations which have been discovered.

Don't look yet!

When the drawings are finished, have the students turn them over or put them inside their desks. Now it's time to take the object out of the bag, study it again, and draw it lifesize while looking at it. Care should be taken to include every possible detail. It's great fun to compare the two finished drawings and find out whether your hands can see as well as your eyes.

Imagine how exciting this discovery can be, for in some cases the first drawing may not be the same kind of an object or it may be interpreted in a different way. You can also work out an interesting bulletin board for your room or hallway showing the comparative drawings. Texture, total involvement, contour, and just plain fun are yours in this artistic version of Blind Man's Buff.

Make It Easy—for Yourself!

1. Prepare your class in advance by talking about texture and contour of objects.
2. Have each child keep in mind that he wants to fool someone. Try to select objects which will be difficult to recognize by touch.
3. Try to avoid the use of ordinary pencils in drawing. Children are conditioned to write small with pencils and their drawings reflect this.

4. Stress the idea that in both drawings the purpose is to get the object as close to reality as possible.
5. Have all drawing supplies passed out first and all movement such as pencil sharpening taken care of before the bags are distributed.
6. Stress the importance of total concentration while drawing.
7. Have several extra bags with articles in them so the last children may also have a choice of bags.
8. Be sure children bring in only those things which will be safe to handle—no sharp edges.

Variation

Instead of drawing, try making the unseen object out of clay. The importance of form and texture still should be stressed. Simple objects must be used for this lesson.

Variation for Lower Grades

Have a few bags full of materials with different kinds of textures. You may use a bag of cotton, yarn, fabric, stones, grass, sandpaper, or anything else with a distinctive feel. Pass the bags throughout the class having each child reach in to feel—but not see—what's in the bag. With crayons or paint each child makes something that would feel like the texture in the bag.

Lesson Thirteen:

ON AND ON AND ON

String Printing

DON'T THROW AWAY THAT CAN! SAVE IT. Use it to roll your own prints that go on and on and on.

Let's do some printing today—string printing. We'll use empty tin cans for our rollers. Can you figure out a way to print with string and tin can rollers? Surely. Tie a piece of string around a can—like that. Then wrap it around the can. I can wrap it around the can just a few times or many times, depending upon the kind of design I want. Do I have to wind it evenly around the can? No, of course not! I can slant the lines of string as I wind it—or see, I can even cross over some of the other lines as I wind the string around the can. That will add variety to my design. And, when I have enough string on my roller, all I have to do is cut it—and poke the end of it under another part of the string. If yours doesn't seem tight enough to hold, you could even tie a knot in it.

Now the printing cylinder is finished, and you're ready for the part that's fun. But it wouldn't be much fun to get paint all over your hands as you rolled it. That would be a mess, wouldn't it?—and it would spoil your print, too! So how can you roll that tin can without having to get your hands on it? Yes, both ends have been cut off the can, so it will be easy to put your fingers inside each end of the can. Then just press on each side as you roll it. Let's try that.

Spread some tempera paint onto a heavy piece of paper. Lay the can on it, press your fingers down on the inside—and roll it over the inking pad. Roll back and forth in different directions several times to be sure the cylinder is thoroughly inked with paint. There—that was easy, wasn't it! And it will be even easier to print it.

Print on any kind of paper—white or colored. Begin with the can just off the bottom edge of the paper to be printed. Roll it entirely across the paper to just off the top edge. Repeat the process over and over again until the whole page—or as much of it as you want—is filled. Even continue by printing across the page from side to side. Re-ink the cylinder as it is needed.

Continue on and on and on. Then use the pictures as lovely designs—or as such useful objects as placemats and booklet covers.

Make It Easy—for Yourself!

1. Cover all work areas with newspaper. Begin to roll the design on the newspaper, continue across the printing paper, and finish with the roller on the newspaper. This prints the entire surface of the paper. If printing is desired only on certain areas, of course that can be done, too.
2. Use waterbase block printing ink or regular tempera paint.
3. Make an inking pad by putting the ink—or paint—on oak tag or other fairly heavy and non-absorbent paper. Spread it with a tongue depressor or other flat stick.
4. Print on any kind of paper. The size and kind of paper will be determined by what you do with the prints. Use them as designs only—on 9" x 12" or 12" x 18" white or colored construction paper. For placemats you will want 12" x 18" construction paper. For gift wrapping paper use larger, thinner paper—perhaps 18" x 24" newsprint or tissue paper.
5. Clean up the easy way. Throw away the can—string and all. It will be easier to get more cans for another lesson than to clean and save these. Fold the pieces of newspaper, collect them, and throw them away.

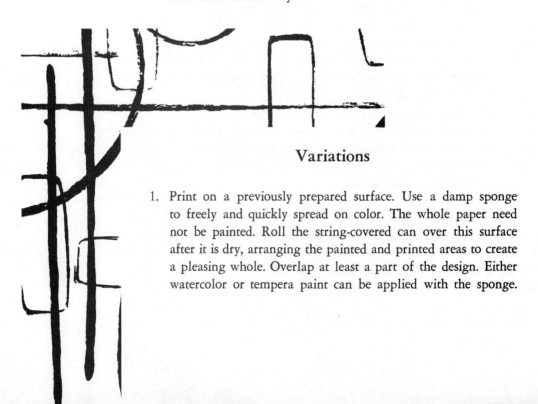

Variations

1. Print on a previously prepared surface. Use a damp sponge to freely and quickly spread on color. The whole paper need not be painted. Roll the string-covered can over this surface after it is dry, arranging the painted and printed areas to create a pleasing whole. Overlap at least a part of the design. Either watercolor or tempera paint can be applied with the sponge.

2. Combine string printing with gadget printing. Print only a part of the paper. Place it so that it creates a rhythmic, moving design. Finish the design by printing with one or two gadgets. The whole paper need not be covered but you will probably want to overlap some parts of the two kinds of printing. Use simple gadgets for printing: the rim of a bottle top, edge of a tongue depressor, paper cup, empty spool of thread, side of an eraser. The gadgets can be pressed into the same inking pad as was used for the string or the color can be painted on with a brush.

OBJECTIVES

1. To make a useful object from materials that are usually discarded.

2. To combine a variety of materials to create an art object.

3. To use texture to create interest.

(For Grades K through 6)

Lesson Fourteen:

IT CAN BE DONE!

Decorated Cans

WHAT DO YOU DO AFTER YOU'VE OPENED a can? If you're like most people, you toss it into the rubbish. Did you know that instead of throwing it away you could make it into a lovely pencil holder, waste basket, or tray for pins or paper clips? Yes, it can be done—with a can!

Decide what you would like to make, and then find a suitably sized can. The most common sizes of cans are wonderful for pencil holders; the giant size juice cans (or the gallon size your cafeteria throws away) make convenient desk waste baskets; even the tiny, almost flat cans come in handy for tray-like containers for small items such as clips or thumb tacks. So decide what you would like to make and find the right can. Or if you prefer, bring in a can and then determine what it is best suited for.

How can you transform that ugly can into a useful and beautiful article? Well, that's easy enough! In fact there are so many ways of doing it, that you'll have to decide on just one for the present. You will need burlap or some other textured fabric, heavy string, and glue. That's all— and when they are put together, you'll have a lovely and practical article from something you almost threw away!

Be sure, first of all, that the entire top of the can has been removed so that there are no sharp or jagged edges. Most electric or safety can openers automatically do this. Then begin by measuring the space between the top and bottom rims of the can. That will be just the flat, round part of the can—not the tiny protruding rims at the top and bottom.

Next, cut a piece of fabric exactly the same width—and long enough to wrap around the can with a half inch or so extra to overlap. What will be an easy way to attach the fabric to the can? Well, we'll use glue so that the cloth will adhere to the metal surface. Just spread a little glue all over the outside edge of the can. Then lay it on its side and place the end of the fabric on the can so that it fits between the top and bottom rim. Turn the can slowly—just a little at a time—as you press the material to it. Be sure it rolls on smoothly. Keep those edges even. There, that was easy, wasn't it?

Now apply just a little glue to the part of the cloth that overlaps, and then press it firmly in place. Looks good already, doesn't it? But there is still one little finishing touch to do.

Just above the bottom rim of the can—and right over the fabric—apply a band of glue. How wide a band? Well, that depends upon the size of the can. For a tiny can, make it a tiny band—perhaps only a quarter of an inch wide. For a little bigger can, make it a little wider, perhaps a half an inch. For a giant can, make it a giant band, perhaps as much as an inch wide. On this glued area we are going to wind some heavy wrapping cord, so you decide how wide you want it to be.

Will the border of cord or twine look good if it is wound loosely and unevenly? Of course not! So lay the end of the cord as close to the rim of the can as you can get it. Hold it there tightly while you wrap the can once, twice, or more times—depending on how wide a border you want to make. Cut the cord and press the end firmly into the glue. Even spread a speck of glue on top of the cut end of cord and smooth the edges. Hold it securely until the glue begins to set.

There, the bottom edge looks good—much better than the top, doesn't it? Well, that's easy to fix—just repeat the process along the top rim of the can. Then sit back and admire your masterpiece. See, it can be done—with a can!

Make It Easy—for Yourself!

1. Burlap or other heavily textured materials create more pleasing effects than smoother fabrics.
2. Have a variety of colors to choose from. Encourage each child to choose a color which will be appropriate to the setting in which the finished article will be used.
3. Use heavy cord or wrapping twine to wind around the can. It will be easier to use and more effective than thinner string.
4. If the glue does not have a brush applicator, make a spreader out of scrap paper. Simply fold the paper several times, then bend it in half to strengthen it.
5. Cover all work areas with newspaper to protect them from the glue.
6. Use glue rather than paste. Paste will not adhere to metal.
7. Be sure the cloth is cut the exact size of the area between the top and bottom rims of the can. Press the cloth smoothly against the can, removing all wrinkles and keeping the edges even.

Variations

1. Make a regular fingerpainting. Cut a strip from it to wrap around the can.
2. Marbleize a piece of paper to glue to the can. To marbleize paper fill a large, rectangular pan (a large cake pan or cookie pan is good) with a small amount of water. Drop several colors of enamel paint on the surface of the water. Use a stick to gently move the colors into pleasing lines that curve and move about. Then lay a piece of paper on top of the whole thing. Remove it—and there is a reproduction of the swirling lines that were on the water, a marbleized paper.
3. Create a color collage on the can in the same way as you would on a flat surface. Decide on one or more colors for your collage. Choose several varieties of the colors in different textures. Have both scraps of paper and cloth available. Overlap them as they are glued to the outside of the can. Make some areas large and others small.
4. Use cotton roving or bulky yarn to cover the whole outside of the can. Begin winding it close to one rim of the can and continue round and round to the opposite rim. Be sure the two ends of yarn are held firmly in place until the glue begins to harden.

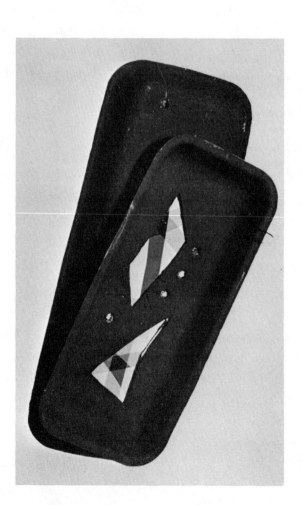

OBJECTIVES

1. To make a decorative object from a throw-away item.

2. To learn to use simple shapes to create a pleasing design.

3. To appreciate contrast of surface textures.

(For Grades 5 and 6; adapted to Grade 4)

Lesson Fifteen:

HYPNOTIZED

Traymobiles

SLOWLY TURNING, THIS WAY AND THAT WAY—BACK and forth, back and forth—swaying gently, moving slightly. Don't watch it too long or you'll be hypnotized!

What is it that almost hypnotized you? Just ordinary papier-mâché trays that came from the grocery store. When you brought them home from the market they had oranges in them—or perhaps grapes, or squash, or some other kind of food. But not any more! Now they are delightful mobiles with brightly colored see-through designs.

Collect the necessary materials and have them ready in advance. All you'll need will be two papier-mâché food trays for each person, glue, black tempera paint, and bits of colored cellophane. Let your class gather around you while you discuss how to make the traymobiles.

Papier-mâché trays are good for holding things, but they aren't very pretty, are they? Well, we can do something about that. If we made a hole in the bottom of the tray it would look better. Oh, it won't hold food any more, but we don't care about that any longer! Do you think the shape I cut should be a fancy one or a plain one? No, I'm going to make a very plain, simple shape. It would be difficult to cut a fancy shape—and besides, a simple shape will look better on such a small area.

While you are talking, cut a freeform or simple geometric shape. Push a hole through the tray with the point of the scissors first, then work outward from it until there is a pleasing shape. There, that's big enough. I mustn't go too close to the edge of the tray because I'm going to cover it with a piece of cellophane, so I'll need an edge around my hole to make a place for the glue. And of course I don't want any ragged edges, so I'll carefully trim off that rough edge.

Make one or two more shapes—depending upon the size tray you have. Stress the importance of leaving plenty of solid space between the shapes. Why? For several reasons: the cardboard would probably tear if the spaces were too close together, you need space to glue the cellophane, and solid space makes a pleasant contrast with the open areas.

61

Perhaps there are some solid areas too large to leave plain and too small to cut open shapes into them. Can you think of some way of adding tiny areas? No, you can't cut little bits of shapes. Scissors just won't cut tiny things from a material as heavy as this. But do you remember what I did when I first started my shapes? Right! I made a little hole with the closed points of my scissors! I'll do that again. But this time I won't cut a shape out—I'll just . . . ? Right again! I'll twist the scissors back and forth a little until I have a small round hole just the right size. But one round hole all by itself doesn't look right, does it? So I'll just find another place and make two or three more.

Don't overdo your design. Remember—a few simple but well planned shapes will look better than many crowded together. Hold your design up to the light. The light areas against the solid areas make a pleasing contrast. Eventually we're going to make a mobile, and we will need two trays with exactly the same designs on them. How can we make another one just like this? Surely, that is easy! Just lay another papier-mâché tray under this one and trace the design. Be sure, of course, that the second tray is turned upside down so that the two backs are together. We'll glue them together later.

There are a few more things you can do to make the design look even better. Place a piece of colored cellophane in back of the cut-out design and again hold it up to the light. Isn't that lovely! Now, if the solid part of the papier-mâché tray were a dull black, what a nice contrast it would make—bright and dark colors, dull and shiny finish. That's really very easy to do—just paint the front and sides of each tray with black tempera paint.

The paint will dry quickly, and then you can glue colored cellophane to the back of one of the designs. Now can you see why we made two trays just alike? We can glue the two of them together so that the edges of the cellophane are hidden, and our lovely design will look finished on both sides.

All that's left to do is insert a thread through a hole in the top and suspend the design as a mobile—a traymobile. Now sit back and admire it as it sways gently, turning slightly—but don't watch it too long or you *will* be hypnotized!

Make It Easy—for Yourself!

1. No pencils—let the scissors form the shapes.
2. Cut only two or three large shapes.
3. Leave a wide space between the shapes—to prevent tearing, to allow space for the glue, and to create a more pleasing contrast.

4. If you have two trays of different sizes, cut the design into the smaller one first.
5. Use extra care punching holes through the tray with the scissors. Keep the scissors closed to form a single point. Press gently but firmly until there is a hole, and then rotate the blades to increase the size and keep the opening round.
6. Have one punched hole near the top of the tray so that later it can be suspended as a mobile.
7. Be sure to reverse the second tray before tracing the design onto it. The backs of the two trays should be together in the same positions as they will be glued.
8. Paint the trays before glueing the cellophane.
9. Glue the cellophane. Paste will not adhere to it.

Variations

1. Use paper or plastic cups in a similar way.
2. Glue aluminum foil to each tray instead of the cellophane. Mount each individual tray (not double as for the mobiles) on a black paper background to form a class mural. Fit the various sizes and shapes of the trays together to create an abstract pattern, letting the black paper background show between each design.

Variation for Lower Grade

Cut simple designs from black construction paper. Glue colored cellophane (or aluminum foil) to the open areas. Display in a window so that light passes through them, or mount them on white paper for a similar effect.

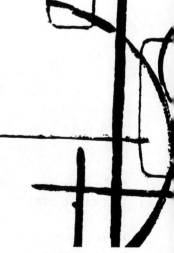

OBJECTIVES

1. To foster imagination through making unreal fun-filled bugs and insects.

2. To show how existing shapes can be combined in a creative composition.

3. To provide an opportunity for selection of materials on an individual basis.

(For Grades 4 through 6)

Lesson Sixteen:

OVER EASY

Egg Carton Sculpture

HOW DO YOU LIKE YOUR EGGS? SUNNY side up? Over well? Scrambled? Poached? Over easy?

How do you like your art? Creative? Fun filled? Imaginative?

You can have both, for after you've enjoyed your eggs you can use your egg cartons for a delightful art project. There is one catch. Your egg cartons have to be papier-mâché—you know, the strong waterproof kind with individual cups and a flip top. If you don't have this type, your students can bring them in from home, or the local luncheonette can save them for you. They're very handy as paint containers, and they're lots of fun as a sculpture material.

Egg carton sculpture may take many forms from abstract to realistic. In this case let's try some make-believe bugs or insects. These may be used as a springtime motif or used to correlate science and art. In either case, they're fun and easy to do.

Ask your class to name and describe the different parts of insects—legs, bodies, stingers, antennae, eyes, wings may be mentioned and talked about. How would an insect from another planet look? Who knows? But wouldn't it be great fun to invent some? We aren't confined to what we know, for we can imagine all kinds of things. Maybe our bug could have two heads or five wings or one large eye, or two sets of antennae or even four tails. Let's see how strange or how beautiful we can make them.

Some students may want to use a whole carton for the body. Others may want to break off two cups for their body. It doesn't really matter, for our imagination is our only guide. The cartons can be used with the tops on or off, used in pieces, used upside down, used plain or painted, or used in conjunction with other materials.

When the body has been designed, other parts may be made from the cartons. The individual cups make great pop eyes when attached upside down. Legs, antennae, and stingers can also be formed by cutting and glueing the cartons. Wings can be made from the flat tops.

65

If possible have available a lot of assorted materials such as pipe cleaners, yarn, buttons, construction paper, newspaper, tissue paper, or old magazines. These materials can lend themselves to a variety of details on our bugs. Beautiful tissue paper wings, curly pipe cleaner antennae, and sparkling jewelry eyes are only a few of the possibilities.

Have fun. Let your class be as imaginative as possible and you will be delighted with the array of fun-filled bugs and insects. Your comment when the class is over?—Easy!

Make It Easy—for Yourself!

1. Use a heavy duty glue to keep the pieces together. The papier-mâché is fairly heavy and may not hold together with paste.
2. Let each child start with a whole carton, then bring the unused portion to a scrap pile so others may use what he didn't want.
3. Try to provide a lot of different materials. These can usually be brought in from home. Separate each group of materials.
4. Staples and pins are also good to have on hand for emergencies.
5. If using glue, cover desks.

Variation

Use only the cartons and glue or staples to have the students create abstract sculptures. These can be displayed separately or combined into a huge class sculpture. They can also be painted or sprayed.

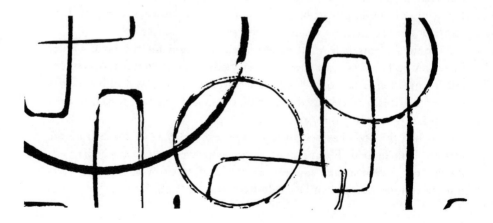

OBJECTIVES

1. To demonstrate basic color theory and make it more understandable.

2. To create a dramatic three-dimensional color "wheel."

3. To use "found" materials to create a three-dimensional design.

(For Grades 4 through 6)

Lesson Seventeen:

A TISKET, A TASKET

3-D Color Wheels

"A TISKET, A TASKET, A GREEN AND YELLOW basket." They're probably green already—just as they come from the grocery store. They had strawberries or raspberries or some other kind of fruit in them then. We're going to make them into three-dimensional color "wheels."

You will need two pint plastic baskets for each child. You've probably kept them—the open kind that looks almost as though it is woven. They looked too good to throw away, but you've never found a use for them. Well, bring them out now—then get some glue and bits of colored cellophane. You'll need the primary colors (red, yellow, blue).

Start by holding a piece of colored cellophane up to the light. Pretty, isn't it, as the light goes through it! Hold up a second primary color next to it. Then move the two together until they overlap. Only two pieces of cellophane—but now you have three colors! The blue and the yellow have become . . . ? Green, that's right! (Or the blue and red have become purple, or the red and yellow have become orange.) Overlap the other combinations of primary colors, too. See, with just three pieces of cellophane we can end with six colors. Yes, you can—you can get a seventh color! There where all three primary colors overlap is another color—brown.

Well, we've just been holding them up to the light, but now let's put them together to make a mobile. We'll use our plastic baskets for that. They will be fine, won't they, because the light will go right through the open spaces. Even the design of the basket will be pretty as it shows through the color.

Cut off a strip of cellophane and hold it against the basket to show the color and the design of the basket. Then glue it in place. Cut another piece of the same color cellophane. Make it a different size than the last strip. Find a good area for it—perhaps at right angles to and overlapping the last piece. Hold it up to the light. See—where they overlap it is a brighter color.

Continue placing the same color cellophane on the one basket until there is an interesting pattern of color. It will be all the same color but there will be variations of it where two or even three pieces overlap. Don't overdo it, though. Leave some open areas to make a more pleasing pattern of color and light.

But that's only one color and we must use the three primary colors in order to make all seven colors. How can we do that? Yes, we could put more colors on the same basket, but then the green and orange and purple and even brown would always stay in the same places. Can you think of any way of doing it so that the new colors change places as the mobile moves? We are going to use a second basket, you know. Of course—put a second color on the second basket! The third color? Well, we'll think about that later.

Plan the arrangement of a second color cellophane as carefully as you did the first one. Glue each piece to the second basket, overlapping some, having only single layers in some places, and leaving other parts of the basket uncovered.

Now, we have used two colors. Place the two open ends of the baskets

(on which no cellophane has been glued) together. See the lovely new color! And it constantly changes place as the design moves. Isn't that better than glueing the two colors together?

But there's just one trouble. That's right—we haven't used the last of the three primary colors. Can you think of any place to put that so that it will make the other colors change, too? Probably someone will suggest putting it between the two baskets. So cut two or three strips of cellophane and glue them to the open end of one of the baskets. Be sure to leave some of the area uncovered. Last of all glue the tops of the two baskets together. When the glue is thoroughly dry, tie a thread to one corner and suspend your mobile.

You may have spoiled the jingle about a green and yellow basket, but your "a tisket, a tasket" has taken on new beauty. You'll be fascinated as you watch new shapes and new colors formed from a gently turning color "wheel."

Make It Easy—for Yourself!

1. Cover all work areas with newspaper before using glue.
2. Give each child a small piece of cellophane (about 4″ x 8″ is ample) of each of the three primary colors—yellow, blue, red.
3. Cut edges of cellophane smoothly, as any variations will show on the finished designs.
4. All colors of cellophane may not make new colors equally well. If a color is too light to change effectively, it may be strengthened by overlapping it with the same color.
5. Leave some open areas on the basket for contrast and design.
6. Save the open ends of the baskets for the third color of cellophane.
7. Plastic baskets are fragile, so warn children to handle them carefully.

Variations

1. Combine several of the individual mobiles into a group mobile.
2. Use colored tissue paper instead of cellophane.

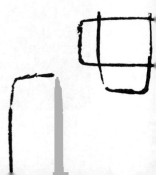

from the

LIVING ROOM DINING ROOM

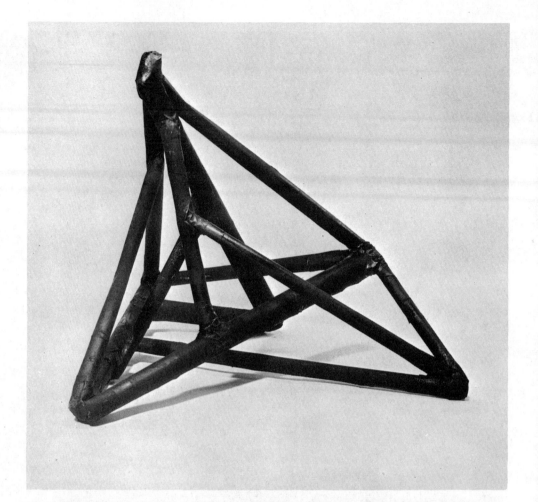

OBJECTIVES

1. To create three-dimensional line structures.

2. To use line to create a moving, rhythmic pattern.

3. To afford an opportunity to learn about balance in a three-dimensional design.

4. To help to understand the importance of space in a design.

5. To see the possibilities for using a common two-dimensional material to create a three-dimensional design.

(For Grades 4 through 6; adapted to Grades K through 3)

Lesson One:

ROLL, ROLL, ROLL YOUR OWN

Rolled Newspaper Structures

Roll, roll, roll your own,
Make them good and strong!
Merrily, merrily, merrily, merrily—
Roll them short or long.

WHAT ARE YOU
going to roll? Why, newspaper, of course. We are going to make three-dimensional structures. All you will need will be newspapers—lots of them —and some paste. Wheat paste, the kind you use for papier-mâché, will be fine.

How can we make newspapers strong enough to make a strong, three-dimensional structure from them? Why, just roll them! We'll begin by taking a couple of double sheets of newspaper. Fold them in half—as though they were a single page. Now begin at one end—top or bottom—and roll them into a tight, strong tube. Make another one—and another—and another. Each time you make a tube or roll, hold it firmly together by pasting a short strip of newspaper around each end and around the middle.

But, of course, any structure you make will need rolls of different lengths, so—make some of different lengths. If you want a giant structure, use several full sheets of newspaper rolled together. For shorter rolls, cut the newspaper into smaller pieces—the length you want your rolls to be. Each time hold them firmly together with strips of pasted newspaper. Continue to roll, roll, roll your own—until you have ten or twelve of them.

Now let's put them together into an interesting three-dimensional structure. Arrange three or four rolls together to form a flat base. Wherever you want to connect two rolls, just attach them by putting a pasted strip of newspaper around them. Make it cross and go over and under them in all directions. Use a second or even a third pasted strip. You want the connection to be as strong as any other part of the roll of paper.

There—you have a beginning, but how can you add height to your base—make it into a structure? That's right! Just add some rolls upward

73

from the base. Attach two more rolls to joints—or in between joints—on the base. Bring them together at the top to form an inverted V. Paste strips of paper around them to hold them firmly together.

Continue to add to your structure. Certainly! One roll of paper may extend right through the open area created by other rolls of paper. That will make your structure more interesting, won't it?

Perhaps you need to make more rolls by now. Well, that's easy. Just decide how long you want them to be. That will depend upon where you are going to put them, won't it? Use enough newspaper to make the rolls sturdy but not bulky. Each roll should be firm and strong but not so thick that it is heavy or hard to attach to another roll.

Frequently turn your structure so that you see it from all sides. Three-dimensional designs should look good from all sides, shouldn't they? Once in a while step back away from your structure. That will help you see it better so that you can decide what to do next.

Walk about the room offering suggestions, answering questions, helping wherever there is a problem. Does your structure begin to look out of balance? Perhaps something added to the other side would balance this long line. All the lines of your structure are about the same length—makes it look a little monotonous, doesn't it? Could you find a place to add a shorter roll? Of course, you could change the shape of the area by extending a line through it. Stand back and look at your structure. What could you add to make it more interesting? Make those joints strong! Paste two or three strips of newspaper around them in all directions.

Finally the last strip will be attached—each structure will be complete. Let them stay on the desks while groups of children take turns walking about the room to look at each design. Then carefully put them to one side so that they can dry thoroughly.

When they are completely dry they will be much stronger and can be handled safely. Some of the smaller and lighter ones might be suspended and displayed as mobiles.

Make It Easy—for Yourself!

1. Have an ample supply of clean newspaper. Place it in several parts of the classroom so that it will be readily available.
2. Give each child a shallow container of thin paste. Aluminum pans that frozen pies come in make handy containers for the paste. After the lesson they may be thrown away or easily rinsed off and saved. Wheat paste—like that used for papier-mâché—is easier to use than the thicker library paste. It will be easy

to spread the paste on with your hand, press the strips of news-paper over the joint, and wipe the excess paste on the next piece of newspaper before rolling it.

3. Make several rolls of paper before attaching any. Have several sizes on hand.

4. Clean up the easy way. Have one child collect all the pans of paste. If they are to be thrown away, pile them together, roll in newspaper, and discard. If they are to be saved, scoop out the excess paste, wash them in a sink, dry them, and stack them for future use. Have each child fold his newspaper twice and let one child collect them all.

Variations

1. Gather together tubes of various sizes—mailing tubes, cores from paper towels or toilet tissue. Use them in the same way as the rolls of newspaper to create three-dimensional constructions.

2. Make constructions from applicator sticks—or toothpicks. Glue them together. The structures may be left this way, or wet plaster-of-paris may be poured over them. It will cling in un-even areas and add texture to the design. A tiny amount of tempera paint may be added to the water that is mixed with the plaster. It will tint the mixture and add color as well as texture.

Variation for Lower Grades

Use toothpicks, applicator sticks, or even pieces of macaroni to make a three-dimensional construction. Hold the parts together with small lumps of non-hardening clay rather than attempting to glue them.

OBJECTIVES

1. To provide an opportunity to work on a three-dimensional group project.

2. To have the experience of working on a larger-than-life figure.

3. To provide an opportunity to work directly in a semi-fluid material.

4. To learn to use papier-mâché to make a three-dimensional figure.

(For Grades 1 through 6)

Lesson Two:

IT'S A GIANT!

Papier-Mâché

"IT'S A GIANT!" CERTAINLY, IT IS A GIANT—ANY-thing as big as that has to be! It won't be made in a day, of course—but then, what giant is?

Just what kind of a giant are you going to make? Why, any kind at all! Perhaps the time of year will determine that: a snowman, a rabbit, a bird; or perhaps a dog, an elephant, a horse—for any time of year. And what are giants made of? Well, that's hard to say, but this giant will have papier-mâché skin over a chicken wire skeleton.

After you have decided what kind of giant you are going to make, take a large piece of chicken wire and twist it into a big oval for the body. Then think what kind of head your giant should have. Is it a little head on a long neck for a giraffe, or a big head with a long trunk for an elephant, or a small head with a pointed beak for a bird, or just a round ball for a snow-man's head? Whatever it is, twist another piece of chicken wire into a shape that resembles it. Hold the parts together and firmly in place by tying them with a twisted length of wire. Do the same thing for the legs of an animal or the wings of a bird. Give the wire skeleton a pull here or there to round it a little more at that spot—or push it to flatten an area. There, the skeleton is finished, and you are ready to give it a papier-mâché skin.

Prepare the papier-mâché materials ahead of time. You will need a table on which to put your giant—or you may move several desks together to form a table area. Cover it with at least two layers of newspaper so that no paste will soak through them. Have another pile of newspaper to use for the "skin." Last of all you will need a large can of thin wheat paste and a couple of paper plates on which to put the wheat paste.

Choose three or four children to begin making the giant, but let every-one watch while you demonstrate. Tear off a piece of newspaper about the size of your hand. Dip one hand in the paper plate of paste and quickly spread it over the torn piece of newspaper. Now lay the paper over the wire form. Looks like a patch, doesn't it? But there isn't anything there to stick the patch to, so to keep it from falling off we'll just curl the ends

77

around the wire. See, that will hold it right there. Repeat the process several times, each time adding a new patch.

Then let the first group of children begin putting on their own patches. That's the way to do it! Put on plenty of paste and then curl the ends around the wire so the patch won't fall off. Always keep your hands over the giant while you are putting paste on the newspaper so that if any falls off, it will land on him and not on the floor.

After each child has had a chance to add several patches, let another group of children put on several pieces of newspaper. In a short time the whole giant will be covered with patches of newspaper put close together but not touching each other.

But this is only the beginning of our giant. Now we have to cover every bit of him. That's even easier, though, than what we have already done, because now there is something to stick the paper to. Cover another torn piece of newspaper with a generous amount of paste. Then lay it on your giant so that it overlaps some of the patches that are already there. See, now the paper stays right where it is put, and I don't have to curl under the edges—just flatten them down as smoothly as I can. Rub your hand back and forth over the paper you have just added. That puts a layer of paste on top of the newspaper, too, and helps to smooth all the edges.

Again let groups of children take turns adding papier-mâché to the giant. Continue working on him for as long as you like. Eventually he should have five or six layers of paper in order to make him strong. Make the final layer with pieces of torn paper towel for a good finished surface.

When at last your giant is thoroughly dry and the day has arrived for him to be painted, there will be new excitement. Decide what you want him to look like. Do you want him to be realistic? Or would you like him better if he were an unusual color, if he had stripes or dots or flowers—or some other unusual thing on him? Well, you decide—then paint him with your regular tempera paints.

It's a giant, all right—the biggest, most wonderful giant anywhere. He's your very own giant, and there's not another one like him in the whole world!

Make It Easy—for Yourself!

1. Cover all work areas thoroughly with newspaper—at least a double layer.
2. Use wheat paste (powdered wallpaper paste) rather than the regular moist paste. Mix it by adding it to water, stirring continuously, until it is a little thinner than mayonnaise.
3. Pour paste from mixing container into paper plates or disposable

aluminum plates. They are wide enough to be easy to use without spilling.

4. Tear (don't cut) the newspaper into pieces small enough to be easy to handle—approximately the size of your hand. Irregular pieces of paper are better than strips. The edges lay smoother and take the shape of the object more readily.

5. Use plenty of paste. Spread it liberally over the piece of paper. After applying the pasted paper to the object, smooth it down with the palm of your hand. Paste will be on top of the paper as well as under it. This serves two purposes: it helps to smooth and keep the edges flat, and it adds strength to the object when it is dry.

6. When putting the first layer of paper over the chicken wire, apply it in patches. Curl the edges under the wire to help to hold them in place. They will form the base for the first full layer of papier-mâché.

7. Five or six layers will be plenty for a strong papier-mâché object. It will be easy to see when a layer has been applied over the entire object if the layers are alternately made of regular newspaper and colored comic sections. The final layer should be towel paper to give a smooth surface on which to paint.

8. No paste should get on the floor if children are frequently reminded to do all work over the papier-mâché object. Then if any paste drips from their hands it will land where it can be used rather than be a nuisance.

9. It is good "insurance" to have children wear a smock when working. A man's old shirt—with sleeves cut off—worn backwards makes a fine smock.

10. When the finished papier-mâché object is thoroughly dry, it can be painted with regular tempera paint.

11. Older children will be able to make the wire skeleton. For younger children you should prepare it ahead of time.

Variations for Upper Grades

1. Make smaller, individual papier-mâché objects. For the smaller objects a base of crumpled or rolled newspaper is sufficient. Boxes and cardboard cores may also be used for the framework. When the object is finished, details may be added with felt, buttons, yarn, or other appropriate materials.

2. Make a large, freeform "sculpture." Plan open areas that extend through the form to create a feeling of space. Add areas of crumpled newspapers to build the design out in desired areas.

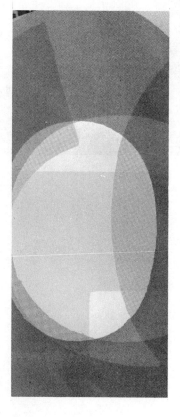

OBJECTIVES

1. To create a new and exciting effect through the use of an ordinary material.

2. To utilize predetermined areas in an original composition.

3. To create an awareness of design as used in commercial areas.

4. To provide opportunity to work on a group project.

(For Grades 2 through 6)

Lesson Three:

"EXTRA! EXTRA! READ ALL ABOUT IT!"

Newspaper Pictures

"EXTRA! EXTRA! READ ALL ABOUT IT! Teacher creates exciting art work in classroom!"

These headlines could apply to you. Unique children's art work can be achieved with very little effort when you supply your class with newspaper. That's right, newspaper—plain, ordinary, everyday newspaper. This time don't use it to cover desks or to wrap trash or to use for current events. This time use it as a background for art work. There are a lot of ways to use newspaper effectively, and one of the easiest is to create a newspaper mural.

Because you are trying to be different and unique, forget two things. Forget about stark realism, and forget that you're working with newspaper. Try to be objective about your medium. In other words, study the paper with an open mind and analyze what's before you. Ask your class what their paper would remind them of if the writing and pictures were designs made by an artist. Point out how the paper is designed with geometric shapes— rectangles and squares. Hold the paper sideways or upside down to point out the design qualities. Point out how areas are made more interesting by the use of large blocks of pictures and advertisements. Compare the classified pages with the feature sections and notice how one is gray looking while the other is broken up with spots of black and white. See how many ideas you can bring out as to how these pages could be used for a picture.

Someone may suggest that the pages with only print on them could be used as a background in a painted picture of a cloudy day. It may also be suggested that combining the dark areas with the white spaces may be used as a cut paper picture on a colored background. These ideas are good and may be used with great success, but there's one more idea that's really very dramatic. The gray quality of the newspaper seems to suggest the color and texture of cement, and the strong vertical lines of the columns seem to suggest the bold, straight lines of modern buildings—so how about a great big mural depicting a city of the future?

81

Give each child a few pages of newspaper, or let each one bring in his own complete paper. Talk about the look of modern buildings, and try to have some pictures of contemporary skyscrapers. Notice how simple the shapes are, how decoration is rarely used without a purpose, how some have an open space under the building for a park-like setting, how much repetition there is in the rows of windows and shafts, how some buildings have a long, low structure combined with a tall tower, how some have a new and different shape made of curves and angles. You'll be happily surprised at the excited response of even young children about futuristic buildings.

Now it's time to turn the excitement into thought. With scissors, have each child design his own buildings, using the columns and pictures of the newspaper. Buildings can be made of one, two, three, or more columns, or parts of columns. Four short columns can be the base of the building with a tall tower of one or two columns. Tops of buildings can be cut into an exciting angle or curve. There are many variations, and after the first attempt the students will get more original.

Details may be added by cutting out dark areas of pictures for windows and doors. If more is needed, black paint or crayons can be used to make slender shafts, windows, doors, promenades, balconies, or anything else the artists thinks of.

Have a large piece of black paper ready for your background. It should be large so one building from each child can be used. This background may be put on a bulletin board so the buildings can be pinned on as soon as they are completed. Or, if a more permanent mural is desired, the background can be spread out on the floor or a table, and the buildings pasted to it. Let each child select one of his buildings to be used for the mural. He then can go to the background and place it where he thinks it will look best. Or you may put them on the background. Some of the buildings will be overlapping, so place the first ones near the top of the paper. Choose buildings with interesting lower floors to go up last and in front of other structures.

The results will be a dramatic semi-abstract version of a city sky line of the future. You will almost hear the headlines—Extra! Extra! Read all about it!

Make It Easy—for Yourself!

1. Have your background ready so that the finished buildings can be put up immediately.
2. Preliminary collections of pictures of modern buildings should be brought in by the class and displayed.

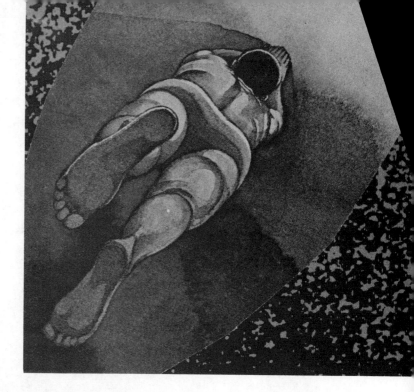

3. Have the children select only one page of newspaper at a time to cut and design their buildings. Other paper can be stored in the desk or under the chair for easy access.
4. Pass out scissors, paste, paint, or crayons before actual work begins.
5. Paint can be distributed in paper cups or on a piece of paper for easy clean-up. Very little paint should be used.
6. Different sizes of newspapers may be used, but avoid colored papers. Black and white contrasts more effectively.
7. Dark colors, other than the black, may be used for a background. This, of course, lessens the dramatic effect of black and white.

Variations

1. Use the newspaper as a background for a painting lesson, incorporating any photographs or ads into the finished picture.
2. Make a black and white cut paper picture by using the different types of print and photographs for texture. For example, tiny print can become a blouse, and a dark skirt can come from a photograph. The mast head of the paper may become part of a sailboat.

OBJECTIVES

1. To provide opportunity for selection of parts to be put in an original picture.

2. To increase ability to arrange parts of a picture.

3. To realize that there may be realistic parts to a picture without the whole picture being realistic.

(For Grades 3 through 6; adapted to Grades K through 2)

Lesson Four:

BE A CUTUP!

Montage

DID YOU EVER WANT TO BE A CUTUP? WELL, NOW'S your chance! It will be fun, too! You won't really have to be a showoff, either. Instead you can show off your cut up picture when you have finished.

All you will need are a pile of old magazines, scissors, paste, and a piece of 12″ x 18″ paper. What would you like to have your cut up picture —your montage—be? Have your class gather around you and we'll see what ideas we can get.

Thumb through a magazine. Look at that big circular piece of machinery. Looks like a big cog of some kind, doesn't it? And there's a picture of two men in overalls. Do they give you an idea? Surely, someone could make a machinery montage. That would be a good beginning, wouldn't it? The cog is much larger than the men. Does that make any difference? No, of course not. In a montage it isn't important that things be in proportion— just that everything is related to one idea. If you wanted, you could use these pictures—or parts of them—to begin a montage.

But let's see what else we can find. Um-m, look at that roast turkey! Looks good enough to eat, doesn't it? How about a food montage! Let's see if we can find anything else good to eat. Oh, there's some ice cream. And look! Grapes and macaroni! That kind of montage would make us hungry, wouldn't it?

Continue to find other things: pets, furniture, cars, houses, bridges. Tear out pages that have pictures of anything that appeals to anyone. Soon there will be more than enough ideas.

Now all that has to be done is find other pictures that have similar things, and then put each idea together into a picture. Let each child have a magazine or two. The sound of tearing pages will assure you that plenty of pictures are being found. Of course you may exchange magazines when you have finished with them.

You must have more than enough pictures by now. What are you going to do with them? Why, put all yours together into one big picture—a

85

montage. No, they don't all have to be facing in the same direction. Put them in any place, any direction just as long as they look good. Some can be upside down, others sideways. Arrange the colors so that they blend together—or so that there is a sharp contrast. Plan the lines of your picture so that your eyes move easily from one place to another. Overlap all the parts of your montage and cover the whole paper. Don't let there be any empty places.

Perhaps you will want to find one word—or several of them—that will fit the subject of your picture. They would be good to put in your montage, too. Arrange them right in with your pictures—upside down, sideways, any place that looks just right.

Give each child newspaper to do his pasting on, paste, and a paste brush. Watch the montages begin to take shape. Aren't all your pictures small? Could you find something that is big? Something large would help to cover the paper in a hurry and make your montage more interesting, too.

Is it necessary to cut out exactly around the outline of each object? No, of course not. Perhaps you will want to leave the background showing on some of them. Perhaps you will want to use only parts of other pictures. You can get lots of variety that way.

That is a good place to use a word in your montage. It makes a nice change, doesn't it? Can you find a different word that could belong to your picture? Perhaps it will be a different color or a different kind of lettering.

86

Continue to help children with their pictures until each montage is finished. What a wonderful bunch of cutups they will be—each one worth showing off!

Make It Easy—for Yourself!

1. Have an ample supply of magazines—at least two per child. These can then be exchanged. Be sure there is a variety of types of magazines so that there will be a wide range of ideas.
2. Stress the importance of having a variety of sizes to the parts of the montage. Start with the larger pieces and overlap them with the smaller ones.
3. Do the pasting on a newspaper so as to keep the montage clean. Fold a page of newspaper so that it will take less space on the desk. Reverse the fold when a clean newspaper is needed.
4. If paste brushes are not available, have the children make paste applicators by folding a piece of scrap paper several times and then bending it in the middle.
5. Clean up the easy way. Pile all the scraps on top of the newspaper and let two or three children collect the piles of scraps and discard them. Do not crumple the papers—just make a pile of them.

Variations

1. Make a large group picture or mural.
2. Have only a part of the montage made up of pictures. Use plain colors and textured materials to complete the picture—cloth of various kinds, corrugated paper, sandpaper, wallpaper.
3. Make a montage from related words (for example: food, cook, fruit, ham, stove, frozen). Fill the rest of the picture with color and texture.

Variation for Lower Grades

Cut out pictures of similar things and paste them on a colored paper—as an individual or class project. Do not attempt to cover the whole paper with pictures. Let the colored paper serve as a background to unite all the parts.

OBJECTIVES

1. To understand and appreciate mosaics as an art form.

2. To have experience making a mosaic—creating a whole from small, individual pieces.

3. To learn to simplify a picture.

4. To appreciate and use "found" colors in a personal way.

(For Grades 3 through 6)

Lesson Five:

JIG SCISSOR PICTURE!

Paper Mosaics

YOU'VE PUT JIGSAW PUZZLES TOGETHER, HAVEN'T you? It's fun, too. It will be even more fun making a jigsaw picture. You won't need a saw—just a pair of scissors. So let's call it a jig scissor picture!

Talk with the class for a few minutes about mosaics. Perhaps they have seen pictures of mosaics in Greece or Rome or other ancient civilizations. Sometimes they covered whole walls or even floors. Sometimes furniture was made as mosaics. Usually mosaics were made of stone or glass or wood, but they could have been made of anything. Whatever the material, small pieces of it were fitted close together with a thin separation of plaster or mortar.

In modern times mosaics are becoming increasingly popular. Perhaps your school has a mosaic. Or maybe there is one on a wall of a nearby supermarket. Someone at home may have a coffee table with a mosaic top. You may have mosaic jewelry. The technique has become so popular that even ash trays are made that way!

But back to our mosaics—our jig scissor pictures. They will be made of paper—paper cut into small pieces and pasted to another paper to form a picture. We'll leave a little space—just a thin line, really—between each mosaic piece. That will let the background paper show and represent the mortar between the pieces.

We're going to find our own colored paper for our mosaics. Give each child a couple of magazines and take time to thumb through the pages. Wherever there is a colored page (advertising is wonderful!) or even a small colored picture, tear it out. Before long you will find that each child has a good assortment of colors. Don't overlook that red automobile— it's a wonderfully bright color. The yellow tile in that picture is just fine. The variety of color is much better than if it were all the same kind of yellow, isn't it?

Now you're ready to make your picture. What is it going to be? Have you thought of something while you were tearing out colors? Perhaps this first time you had better not try to put many things in it. Keep it simple, with just one object or a few large shapes. Yes, it could be a still life arrange-

89

ment—perhaps just a vase with a couple of apples. A sailboat would be fine. You could make the hull one color and the sail another. Then you could even put in the water and the sky. An animal? Certainly—any kind of animal. But keep it simple.

Let the class talk for a while until everyone has his own idea. Now to the scissors. But wait a minute! Are you going to cut the colored pieces out in the shapes they are already? Of course not—that would be silly, wouldn't it! That red car won't look like a car any more. It will just be little pieces of red paper. It might become a part of the sail in your picture—not an automobile at all! Which will be easier to fit close together—rounded edges or straight edges? Straight edges, of course! So if you start by cutting pieces with only straight edges you will find they fit together better. Oh, you may have to change the shape of some of them—to get the round outside edge of your apple, for example.

As you walk about the room during the lesson, you may give each child a little paste on a piece of scrap paper. Each child also will need a paste brush (or paper applicator). He can use the pages still in one of the magazines to do his pasting on—to keep his picture and desk clean. Watch, too, that children do not cut their colored paper into tiny pieces of paper. These would take far too long to arrange into a mosaic and would be less attractive when finished. Keep them moderately small but not tiny.

It takes much longer to make a mosaic picture than to paint or color one, so plan for plenty of time. You may even want to plan to finish them during a second lesson. In any case, your jig scissor pictures will be well worth it. Even the simplest mosaic object with a contrasting mosaic background will produce a dramatic result.

Make It Easy—for Yourself!

1. No pencils! If you want your class to pre-sketch the picture they are going to make, have them use chalk.
2. Have enough magazines so that each person can have at least two.
3. Let children exchange colored sheets so that they will have the colors they need for their own mosaics.
4. Stress cutting small—not tiny—pieces of colored paper. Tiny pieces take too long to put together. Large pieces of colored paper show too much of the original picture and are less interesting.
5. Collect one of the magazines from each person when he has finished with it. This will eliminate an unneeded material, and therefore, allow more work area.
6. Leave one magazine for each person. He can use the plain pages that are left to do his pasting on in order to keep his picture and desk clean.
7. Use paste brushes if they are available. If you do not have them, make paste applicators. Tear out part of a page of the magazine, fold it several times, then bend it in the middle.

Variations

1. Cut out the shape of a real object—an animal, a person, a boat, a tree. Make it BIG. Cut simple shapes—squares, triangles, or circles—from colored magazine pages. Overlap them on the object.
2. Make a non-objective picture. Divide a paper into interesting shapes and sizes. Finish as a mosaic.
3. Make a large group mosaic picture or mural.
4. Cut pieces of colored floor linoleum into pieces. (It will cut with a pair of scissors.) Glue it to a piece of plywood or masonite. Fill in between the mosaic pieces with grout. (Grout is a powder similar to plaster-of-paris and is easily obtainable from a hardware or paint store. Mix it with water according to the directions on the package.) When the grout is firm, remove the excess with a damp cloth or sponge.

OBJECTIVES

1. To use a common household item in an unusual way.

2. To create three-dimensionally with a two-dimensional material.

(For Grades 2 through 6)

Lesson Six:

DON'T WIPE 'EM OFF—
STICK 'EM ON!

Crumpled Paper Napkins

NO, NO, NO! DON'T WIPE 'EM OFF—
stick 'em on! Does that sound strange? With paper napkins, you're
used to wiping things off. But this time we're going to reverse the process,
we're going to use paper napkins to stick 'em on—stick on the paper
napkins, that is!

What would you like to make by sticking 'em on? Autumn trees in
the fall? Snowmen in the winter? Easter eggs or flowers in the spring?
Birds, animals, clowns any time at all? Well, you decide what it is going to
be. But for whatever you make you will need a big supply of paper napkins.
Have as many colors as you can, too.

Now let's begin. We'll plan our picture by sketching it with crayon
on 12" x 18" Manila drawing paper. One color of crayon will be enough,
and just draw the outline for each part of your object. Oh, no, don't fill
in anything with color. It wouldn't show anyway, but even more important,
the paste and paper napkins wouldn't stick to it as well. So just draw lines.
Make as many changes as you want to until your picture is just the way
you want it to be. Don't worry about those extra lines—the ones you don't
want to use. They will be covered up and won't show, or they will be cut
off if they are outside your object.

When the crayon drawing is finished, cut out the object—the snow-
man, the butterfly, the clown, the apple—whatever it is.

Have your class gather about you while you demonstrate. Sketch an
object—or just a shape—on a piece of paper. Spread a liberal amount of
paste over a small area of your drawing. Then quickly tear off a piece of
paper napkin about an inch and a half or two inches square. Crumple it
a little, then stick it into the paste. Tear off a second square, crumple it,

93

stick it into the paste, and push it up close to the first one. Repeat it a third time, a fourth time, a fifth time. Be sure they are all pushed close together. Doesn't look much like a paper napkin now, does it? Be sure the pieces go all the way to the edge of your picture. Don't let any of the paper or crayon lines show. When you come to where a new color should be, well—just change colors. That's easy, isn't it? And fun, too!

Now everybody to work!

My, but those are tiny pieces. Hadn't you better make them a little bit bigger? That's the way to do it—push them all close together. Use plenty of paste—and get all the edges stuck into it. That really begins to look good, doesn't it! Do you think it would be a good idea to leave out some of those tiny details?

Encourage, question, compliment. Fingers will practically fly as paper napkins are torn, crumpled, and stuck on. Time will fly, too. But all at once pictures will begin to be completed—and what unusual pictures they will be! Display them all—they will be worth it.

Make It Easy—for Yourself!

1. Make the object large. It will be more dramatic when finished than a small one.
2. No pencils! Using a pencil tends to make one draw small, detailed things. For this you need a big, simple object. Do the sketching with one color of crayon. Make as many changes as necessary—they won't show on the finished picture. If so many changes are made that the lines become confusing, sketch the final lines with another color crayon so they will be distinguishable.
3. Plan the color arrangement by numbering the different color areas on the sketch.
4. It will be easier if the small areas are completed first, then the larger areas filled in around them.
5. Complete all areas to be done in one color before going to another color. This will make less traffic to the supply areas, fewer materials on the children's desks, and less tendency to change the plan of the design.
6. As you walk about the room, collect the materials that are no longer needed: scissors, crayons, and scrap paper. This will provide more work areas as well as make the clean-up easier.

Variations

1. Use other materials in the same way: tissue paper, face tissue, toilet tissue.
2. Make the object out of 12″ x 18″ colored construction paper. Fill in only parts of it with paper napkins. The colored paper will form part of the background. Be sure all of the drawing has been done on only one side of the paper. Then turn the picture over to the clean side before adding the crumpled paper —so that no crayon lines will show on the finished picture.
3. Make a more complete picture: landscape, still life.
4. Stick the crumpled paper napkins on both sides of the object for a more three-dimensional effect. Or hang the finished picture as a mobile.

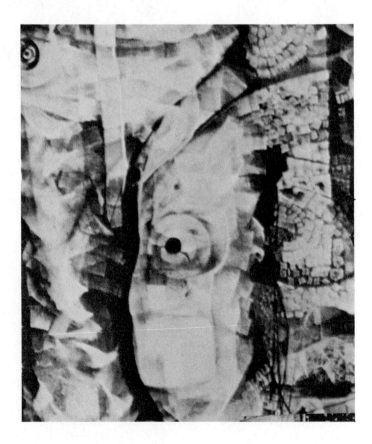

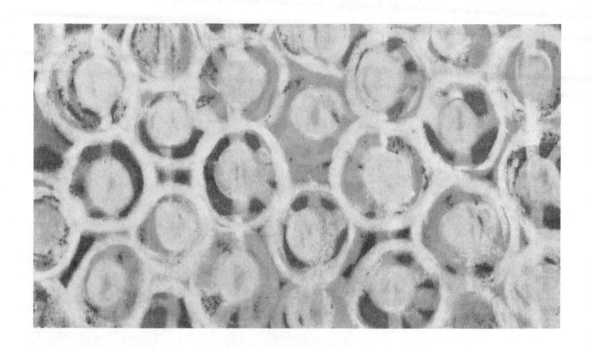

O B J E C T I V E S

1. To learn about an unusual form of textile design.

2. To experiment with a new process of textile printing —batik.

3. To gain a new appreciation for hand crafted work.

4. To see the possibilities for combining common household materials into a new and exciting technique.

5. To see the effect colors have on each other.

(For Grades 4 through 6; adapted to Grades 2 and 3)

Lesson Seven:

NOT FOR LIGHTING

Batik

WHAT WOULD YOU DO WITH CANDLES? PUT THEM ON A BIRTH-day cake? Add a festive note to a dinner party? Use them when the electricity goes off? But for all those things you have to light them. The candles we will use are not for lighting!

We're going to make a batik. Do you know what that is? Batik is cloth designed in an ancient way, and still frequently made in Eastern countries. Wax is used to fill in areas of the cloth so that the dye can't get into those places. Then how do you suppose they get the wax out so that other colors can be used there? Surely, by ironing it out. The heat melts the wax and leaves plain cloth again. The wax may be poured or painted on in other places and the cloth dyed again.

Perhaps someone would like to look up batik in the encyclopedia and find out more about it. Someone may even have some batik at home. You may want to have an exhibit of it—to add to an exhibit of your own made-to-order batik.

But back to how we are going to make batik. We won't have liquid wax that we can paint or pour on. Instead we will use something else that is almost entirely just plain wax. Right! We will use candles. There's lots of wax in them—in fact we call them wax candles, don't we? So the wax for our batik will come from white candles.

If we just rub a candle HARD against the cloth, some wax will come off wherever we have rubbed it. See, like that. It doesn't show much because the cloth and the candle are both white, but the wax is there just the same.

After you have rubbed the candle over several areas of cloth, demonstrate how the dye is applied. Put a small amount of liquid dye in a paper cup. Use it just as you would paint, applying it all over the cloth with a large watercolor brush. Of course, if you were dyeing a large piece of cloth, you would dip it into the dye instead of painting it. If you are using an old piece of cloth that has been laundered many times, the dye will soak into it immediately. But if you are using a new piece of cloth, you may find that you have to rub the brush back and forth several times before the cloth absorbs the dye. See how the dye is pushed off the wax areas! No dye is getting on that part of the cloth, is it?

Now that our first layer of dye is on the cloth, let's get it ready for the next color. To do that we need to get rid of the . . . ? Wax! We'll do that by ironing the cloth. The heat will melt the wax. It will do one other thing, too. It will dry the cloth so that we can paint it with another color.

Take your batik to the ironing area. Lay it on the newspaper and put another piece of newspaper over it. Iron it with a medium hot iron. See how the extra dye is absorbed by the newspaper. Turn the newspaper over and iron the batik again to be sure all the wax and extra dye have been removed. See how nice it looks already—and it has only been dyed once!

What is the next thing to do? Why, wax it, of course! Put wax everywhere you don't want the next color to be. And then what will you do after you have waxed it? Of course, you will paint on another color and then you will iron it to dry it and to remove the wax. And then you will . . . ? Surely, you will wax it again. So it will be Wax, Dye, Iron—Wax, Dye, Iron—Wax, Dye, Iron—over and over again until your batik is finished and beautiful.

Perhaps the first time you make a batik you will want to use just shapes and lines for your design. Of course, if you want to, you may use real objects for your batik. But whatever it is going to be, let's get started. All you will need to begin with is a piece of cloth and part of a white candle.

Urge the children to press hard with their candles so as to leave a heavy coating of wax. While they are doing that, you may give them the other materials they will need—newspaper, a watercolor brush, and a paper cup.

Be sure you put wax on all the areas of cloth where you don't want any dye. That's right! Fill in solid areas where you want the cloth to stay white. Perhaps you will want a different color to be there later. Remember, dye will color any areas that don't have wax on them.

As the children finish their first layer of wax, let them take turns preparing their dye. Then they can paint it onto their pieces of cloth. Oh, be sure to recover *all* the cloth with dye. It isn't like painting a regular picture, you know. It will be as though you dipped the whole piece of cloth into the dye. That's the way we would do it if we were making great big pieces of batik. So fill the whole thing with color because the dye won't be able to get to any parts you have covered over with wax.

The final step is always the ironing. After the dye has been applied, let the children take turns ironing their batik. That's the way to do it! Turn the batik upside down, cover it with another piece of newspaper, and iron it. See how the newspaper becomes colored with the extra dye. Turn the top newspaper over—or take a fresh one—and iron your batik again. This will make sure all the wax is removed. It will also dry the cloth so that you can add more . . . . Wax, that's right! So over and over again it will be Wax, Dye, Iron—Wax, Dye, Iron.

Batik, like almost any handwork, is slow. So plan for plenty of time—you may want to plan several lessons for it. This is no probem at all as the process may be stopped at any point in the Wax, Dye, Iron cycle and then begun at the next point at the next art lesson.

You will be proud to display the finished batiks. Just staple them to a larger plain white paper so as to form a contrast with the dye.

Make It Easy—for Yourself!

1. Talk about how dye is different from paint—that it is a permanent color and will not wash out. This is an advantage on cloth,

but it can create problems unless it is understood and precautions taken. You may want the children to wear old clothes or cover up with an old shirt worn backwards—as "insurance."

2. Keep the supply of dye in one area that is thoroughly covered with several layers of newspaper. Allow only a limited number of children in that area at any one time.

3. Concentrated liquid batik dye (to which each child must add a little water) comes easy to use, but any type of dye can be mixed to form a liquid—then blended with other colors by the children to form their own varieties.

4. An easy way to dispense dye is to put a milk straw in each container of dye. Place a finger over the opening of the straw to lift out a small quantity of dye and transfer it to individual paper cups for blending with water or other colors.

5. Each child should work on several layers of newspaper so that no dye will soak through to the desk.

6. Give each child one paper cup. When he has finished with one color dye, he should empty the remaining dye in the sink (or pail), rinse the paper cup with a tiny bit of water, and reuse it for the next color dye. Because the paper cups are light they tip over easily. Therefore, hold them all the time the dye is being applied to the cloth. Mix enough dye to cover the whole area at a time.

7. The final color of the dye on the cloth will be affected by the

colors under it, so it is well to begin by applying the lightest color which is to be used.

8. Have two ironing areas if possible. A thick pad of newspaper, so that the heat won't penetrate to the desk or table surface, makes a good "ironing board."

Variations

1. Fold or tie the cloth. Dip all or parts of the cloth into one or more colors of dye. When the cloth is unfolded or untied the design will be revealed. Colors will be blended where the cloth was dipped into more than one color.
2. Use wax candles to draw shapes or objects. Make the outlining heavy. Paint the dye into the various shapes. The wax will prevent the colors from running together, and it can later be ironed out of the cloth.

Variation for Lower Grades

Make a picture with wax crayons on cloth. Use one or several colors. Dip the finished picture into dye. When the cloth is pressed, the wax from the crayons will be ironed out but the color from the crayons will be permanent.

from the

BEDROOM

OBJECTIVES

1. To provide a simple, effective form of graphics for the classroom.

2. To introduce printing techniques to young children.

3. To create a more exciting visual effect in a two-dimensional picture.

(For Grades 4 through 6; adapted to Grades K through 3)

Lesson One:

DADDY'S DIRTY SHIRT

Cardboard Graphics

IF DAD TAKES HIS SHIRTS TO THE LAUNDRY
he may be surprised by Junior's happy exclamation about Daddy's dirty
shirt. His son knows that when the shirt comes back there will be a piece
of wonderful cardboard in it. His teacher told him to look for it and bring
it to school. He can't wait because they're going to try something new
in art.

What can you do with these pieces of cardboard? Oh, lots of things.
One of the most rewarding and interesting is printing. Prints have become
increasingly important and popular in the art world and here's an easy way
to show the techniques to children when printing supplies are scarce—or
when the class is too young to handle linoleum blocks, woodcuts, or presses.

Preparation of the printing plate is simple. The application of ink
or paint may vary with what supplies are available. Let's start with the
plate and then go on to various ways of applying ink or paint and the
actual printing process.

All you need to make a plate is a piece of ordinary manila or construction paper, a piece of shirt cardboard or oak tag, scissors, and some
paste. The plate is made the same as you would make an ordinary cut paper
picture. Use the construction or manila paper as the background and cut
and paste the shirt board to make your picture or design. The cut and overlapped pieces of cardboard may not show now since they're all the same
color, but wonderful effects are caused when they are printed. If the board
has a shiny surface (usually white) on one side, make sure this side is up
on your picture. Keep the picture simple with large, uncluttered shapes.
One large object is simpler to cut than many small figures. For example, a
clown's face can be made by cutting out an oval head, then cutting out or
overlapping the eye shapes, a nose, or mouth, overlapping strips for hair,
adding a neck with a large ruffle, and perhaps cutting out or overlapping
polka dots.

When the plate (picture) is finished, it is time to pull a print. If
printing supplies are available, here's what to do.

105

Squeeze out a small amount of waterbase printing ink onto a glass plate, or metal tray, or piece of tile. Take a brayer (roller) and roll it over the ink, spreading it on the glass and covering the brayer. Roll the inked brayer over the cardboard plate (picture). Cover all the cardboard with ink, but try not to get too much on the background paper. Roll it gently and lightly. When the plate is inked, place a fresh piece of paper—contrasting to the color ink—over the plate. Rub it firmly with your hand. Pull off the paper and admire your print! The parts that were cut out are now colored and the overlapped pieces have a halo around them. Some of the background printed, too, but it adds beauty to the print.

If printing supplies are not available try this:

Prepare the plate in the same manner. Instead of ink, try tempera paint. Instead of a brayer use a damp cloth or sponge. Dip the cloth or sponge into the paint and quickly cover the cardboard pieces. Have a piece

of paper ready to put on top of the wet plate. Rub it gently until the paint has transferred to the new paper. Pull off the paper and again admire your print. If you are using paint, the first print may not come out completely because the first layer of paint will soak into the cardboard and dry before you can print it. The next prints should be better. Be careful not to apply too much paint or your print will run and you'll lose your original picture.

Printing is most rewarding and exciting—and Junior will be happy when he sees Daddy's dirty shirt, 'cause he knows he'll get some cardboard for prints.

Make It Easy—for Yourself!

1. Let the paste on the cutouts dry before attempting to pull any prints.
2. Prepare several printing stations in various parts of the room. On tables or empty desks (covered with newspaper) place the ink, glass or tile, and a tube of ink. If paint is being used, place a paper plate or other wide mouth container and a cloth or sponge on the desk.
3. Use these stations only for applying the ink or paint to the plates.
4. The actual pulling of prints should be done at the child's desk.
5. Use construction paper for prints. Any paper too light will tend to stick to the plate and tear.
6. Have each child select his print paper before he inks his plate. This paper should be left at his desk while he is applying the ink or paint to the plate.

Variations for Lower Grades

1. Use the same techniques described in the lesson but have the students cut out geometric or freeform shapes for their plate instead of a realistic picture.
2. Make a plate (picture) out of cardboard on a piece of manila paper. Do not ink it. Place another piece of white drawing paper, tissue paper, newsprint, or manila paper on top of it and rub it with the side of a crayon, chalk, charcoal, or soft pencil. This effect is more like the rubbings of ancient temples, popular in the art market today.

OBJECTIVES

1. To create three-dimensional animal constructions.

2. To correlate realistic animal study with imaginary artistic creations.

3. To use a found material in an art lesson.

(For Grades 3 through 5; adapted to Grades K through 2)

Lesson Two:

IN LIKE A LAMB,
OUT LIKE A LION

Folded Animals

HAVE YOU EVER HAD THE FEELING THAT YOUR class has come into the art lesson like a lamb—that is, meek and mild and unenthusiastic, expecting the same old kind of lesson? If this is your problem, you can make them go out like a lion—"fierce," enthusiastic, and excited. What better way to get a class personally involved with a lesson than having them bring in their own personal supplies!

Tell them to go on a treasure hunt around the house and see if they can find some shirt cardboards from either new shirts or blouses or from shirts coming back from the laundry. Have each child bring in as many as he can in order to compensate for those who cannot find any. When at least one for each child has been collected, have the class bring in any bright "glueable" scraps. These may include pieces of fabric, yarn, colored string, buttons, jewelry, colored pictures, bark, twigs, or anything else that might appeal to the youngsters. If the class is willing, these may be placed in a communal treasure box to be shared by everyone.

It's now time to turn these drab pieces of cardboard into exciting and imaginative creatures. Highly decorated figures of animals, slightly abstract, have become very popular with the public. Ask your class if they have ever seen these delightful creatures made from papier-mâché, or clay, or wood—you know, the kind that are painted in bright sunny colors. Ask them why they think these objects are so appealing. Notice how the artist has designed these creatures. He has given them large expressive eyes or narrow fierce eyes, or droopy sleepy eyes. He has given them a cute expression, a fierce expression, or a sad, sleepy expression. He has sacrificed realism for a decorative effect. Only the subject matter is real. The interpretation is highly unique. This is the approach which should be taken by the students for maximum creative and fun-filled creatures.

The basic technique of construction is quite simple. All you do is take the piece of cardboard, and with the point of an opened pair of scissors score it down the middle. (Draw a line with the point of the scissors.) Fold the board in half along this scored line, and it is now a three-dimensional object very much like the roof of a house—or a pup tent.

Imagine this folded cardboard as the side view of an animal without his head. You'll need to cut out the part between his front and back legs. From the open edges (opposite the fold) cut out a rectangle, leaving the desired width for front and back legs and the body. The doubled cardboard may be too heavy to cut, so cut one side at a time, making sure each side is the same.

Now Leo the Lion or Mary's Little Lamb has a body and four legs. We need heads, tails, ears, and expressions to make our animals unique and personal. Even the cutting of the legs can be original. Instead of a rectangular shape, a curve or a large scallop makes a fat tummy, or a very narrow rectangle suggests a low alligator shape.

Making the head can be approached in several ways. You can cut a slit across the fold above the front legs and insert a round head, or you can cut along the fold and insert a sideview head. Heads can be cut with long necks, short necks, or no necks and inserted in the slits. Faces can be drawn, painted, cut from paper, or made from scraps. Tails can be braided yarn, string, cardboard, fabric, colored paper, or other scraps. Spots, stripes, and shaggy hair can be made in this way, also. Two pieces of cardboard can be used for long, long animals. Cardboard folded the short way can be used for tall animals with long legs or fat animals with short legs.

Don't put any limitations on how the animals must look, and you'll find that if your class comes in as an artistic lamb it'll go out like a creative lion.

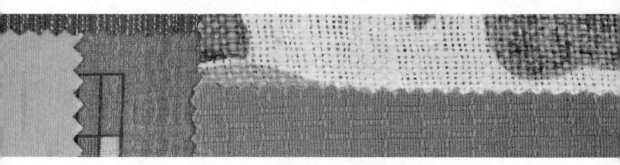

Make It Easy—for Yourself!

1. Keep a collection of "treasures" which have been brought in by the students. You and they will find many uses for them. You will even invent your own lessons.

2. Depending on the size and weight of the cardboard being used, more supports may be needed to keep the animals from collapsing. Under the fold a piece of cardboard may be glued to form a bridge to hold the two sides firm. That's done by taking a small rectangle and folding back the ends. Put glue on the folded ends and attach one end on one side of the body and one end on the other side of the body. If they are placed under the legs these supports will not show.

3. Use a glue—not paste—to join the different parts of the animal.

4. Cover work areas to avoid marring the tops with glue.

5. Make sure enough cardboard is collected before the day of the lesson.

6. Let the children select their embellishments only after they have completed their animal torsos.

7. If space allows, spread the treasures out on a table so all the variations are visible. This will give the children ideas while they are working.

8. Bring in decorative animals—either pictures, stuffed toys, or actual modernistic pieces.

9. Have the children think up names as they work. They may get ideas from the different materials or techniques.

Variations

1. Use construction paper instead of cardboard, but use it double thickness for support.

2. Use this fold technique, but let the class turn the folded board or paper into anything they like. These may be realistic animals and people or way out creatures. The problem to be solved is to turn a folded piece of cardboard into a three-dimensional creative piece. Scraps may also be used in this lesson.

Variations for Lower Grades

1. Fold a piece of construction paper in half. Cut a half circle along the fold. Add a head, wings, and a tail for a delightful 3-D bird.

2. Use the same idea but cut a half oval to create a fanciful fish or insect.

OBJECTIVES

1. To use a new but common material to make a picture.

2. To use cloth in a different way.

3. To increase awareness of pattern and texture in a picture.

4. To increase awareness that a picture may have real things in it even though they do not look completely realistic.

(For Grades 3 through 6; adapted to Grades 1 and 2)

Lesson Three:

BY THE YARD

Cloth Pictures

YOU DON'T HAVE TO MAKE PICTURES THE ORDINARY way with paint or paper or crayons. Be different—make them with cloth. You'll begin with cloth—by the yard if you like, but mostly just lots and lots of scraps. You'll end with a room full of unusual pictures.

Begin by gathering as many varieties of cloth as you can get—big pieces or little pieces, plain colors or printed, smooth or rough material—but as many kinds as you can find. Perhaps you will even find some felt. And it won't be at all hard to add yarn of several colors. The only other materials you will need will be paste and scissors.

Cut some of the larger pieces of cloth in pieces at least 9" x 12" (a little larger would be better if you have pieces big enough). They should be plain colors, some light and some dark. These will be the backgrounds onto which the cloth pictures will be pasted.

Now—what kind of a picture would you like to make from all these things? Do the pieces of cloth make you think of anything? Perhaps some-one will see an animal in one of the prints. Yes, you could make some animals, a whole zoo full of animals. But you wouldn't just cut out that little dog that's on the cloth, would you? No, of course not! That is just a part of the design of the cloth. That just gives you an idea. So you might make tigers, and elephants, and monkeys, and all the animals you would find in a zoo. You could use lots of kinds of cloth for them, couldn't you?

Someone else may think the lovely colors remind him of flowers. Or perhaps a heavy piece of wool reminds another person of a warm winter coat. So he might think of a picture of skiers, or skaters. So lots of ideas will come just from looking at the cloth. Each idea will lead to another one —real things the children have seen or done or read about or things they imagine.

How do you begin a cloth picture? Why, like any other picture. You always make the most important thing first—the thing the picture tells you about. And of course you make it big. So you think about what is most im-portant and you make that first. It might be made from one piece of cloth or you might need several pieces of different kinds of cloth for it. Then you

just fill the cloth background with whatever needs to be a part of your picture. Be sure your picture tells something. We wouldn't want it to be just a few objects.

Pass out scissors and let the pictures begin to take shape. As the scraps of cloth are tranformed into people and pyramids and fish and tractor trucks —and whatever else imaginations can think up—you may give the children paste so they can continue their work. They won't want to pause until their pictures are entirely finished.

When all is completed, you will agree that the cloth as pictures looks much better than when it was just cloth by the yard—or even scraps!

Make It Easy—for Yourself!

1. Have as much variety of cloth as possible—plain and printed, smooth and textured. Have it torn or cut into small pieces about 6" x 9".
2. Arrange the material on a large table or counter space so that children can easily see it in order to make good choices.
3. Have the background material cut before the lesson begins. About 9" x 12" (or larger) is a good size. Use solid color materials, some light and some dark colors. Either smooth textured cloth (like percale) or rough textured cloth (like burlap) make good background materials.
4. No pencils! Cut the cloth without drawing on it.

Variations

1. Make a similar type of picture using a combination of cloth and paper—including newspaper and gift wrapping paper.
2. Make a mural or large wall hanging. It can be a class or group project.

Variations for Lower Grades

1. Make only one or two important things from the cloth. Paste them onto 12" x 18" manila drawing paper. Complete the picture with tempera paint, crayon, or colored construction paper.
2. Make a collage, using a combination of cloth and paper.

OBJECTIVES

1. To transform the beauty of soft fabrics into a bas-relief picture.

2. To combine pattern, color, and texture of fabric into a unique and unified composition.

3. To relieve the monotony of two-dimensional work in the classroom.

4. To create a three-dimensional picture from a normally two-dimensional medium.

(For Grades 4 through 6)

Lesson Four:

DRAPE IT, SHAPE IT

Bas-Relief Fabric Pictures

YOU CAN DRAPE IT, SHAPE IT; PIN it, snip it; fold it, hold it; gather it, lather it—but have you ever pasted it? The "it" is fabric—wonderful, colorful, pliable fabric. Everyone knows the versatility of fabric in our everyday lives and you may have used it in a collage or as an embellishment for a picture. There's another way of handling fabric that is quite different and very effective. In this situation we're going to study the design of the fabric, investigate what the designer was trying to express, and use his designs for our own purposes.

115

Fabrics just don't happen—they are designed by artists! Each fabric has its own personality and its own reason for being. Collect some pieces of material and show the class how each one has been designed with a purpose in mind. You and the class might discover that an artist was trying to show beautiful texture (hopsacking, burlap, bouclé), or perhaps he was trying to show repeat pattern (cotton prints, wool plaids), or perhaps he was trying to capture the elegance of the material by using brilliant, jewel-like colors (silks, satins). In any case, fabric has its own charm, and the problem to solve in this lesson is how to put together the various design elements of fabrics into a bas-relief kind of picture.

The first step, of course, is selecting fabrics. Try to have many different kinds of materials available for a good selection. These may be scraps of materials donated by you and the class. Try to get both solids and prints in your collection. The fabrics may be put into a large box or spread out on a table or counter. Have each child select two kinds of fabrics that he thinks will go well together. One may be a large, splashy print and the other a muted solid color. More fabric may be used during the lesson, but limit the choice at the beginning for less confusion. Large pieces of cloth may be cut up for wider distribution.

When the fabric has been selected, the actual picture-making begins. Use a lightweight cardboard, such as oak tag or thin shirt boards, or construction paper. Spread paste evenly on approximately the same area as the size of the cloth. Adhere the fabric to it (laminate it), and repeat the process with another piece of material. While the fabric is drying, sketch an idea on scrap paper.

Now we must turn our sketch into a bas-relief picture. The easiest way to do this is to draw and cut out separate pieces of our picture. For example, if we were making a blossom, we would turn over our pasted fabric and draw each petal separately—and cut them out one by one. We may want to use our other fabric for leaves, so we turn that over and draw, then cut out our leaves. As the paste dries, our fabric-on-board will tend to curl. This may work to our advantage as it naturally creates a three-dimensional effect.

Choose a neutral background on which to build the finished picture. Black or white is always good. Now we use the cut pieces to form our bas-relief picture. Remember—bas-relief means that the picture must stick up from the background, so in the case of the blossom arrange the petals in a circular formation, pasting down only the ends of each petal, letting the rest of the petal rise from the background. Now add the leaves to enhance the blossom—but again, don't make them flat. Paste down only one end. Other flowers, bugs, or birds in other fabrics may be added for a finishing touch.

There are other ways of making pieces stand up from the background. Cover two ends with paste, but instead of sticking the piece flat, push one end toward the other, causing the center to rise. Pieces may be folded back at one end and pasted, or they may be creased and pasted. Let the class discover other methods of making their pictures rise up from the background.

The cloth which is laminated to the cardboard takes on a different look from ordinary fabric. It assumes the look of being painted. It is also smooth and crisp, and if dry is much easier to cut. The ends don't ravel, so the entire procedure eliminates a lot of the problems pertaining to fabric but keeps the basic beauty of its design.

The finished pictures will not only be unusual because of their three-dimensional effect, but they also will be sophisticated in their appearance. With fabric we don't have to just drape it, shape it—we can also laminate it!

Make It Easy—for Yourself!

1. Start collecting fabrics early so you may ask for specific kinds which do not appear.
2. Don't spread too much paste on the cardboard because it will take too long to dry.
3. Avoid chunks of paste, and smooth out the fabric to get rid of any lumps and wrinkles.
4. Let each piece of fabric dry for a time before trying to cut it. If it is too wet it will be difficult to cut.
5. While one kind of fabric is drying, the student may be allowed to choose and laminate another piece.
6. Have a scrap area in the room so that used fabrics may be put there for others to use.

Variations

1. Paint or crayon a background picture and add the important parts in fabric. For example, a watercolor background of a seascape may be enhanced by a bas-relief sailboat done in a dark olive-green corduroy with a brown cotton mast and snow-white percale sails.
2. Cut out the laminated fabrics in freeform shapes, let them curl, and paste them together to form a three-dimensional abstract sculpture. Try to let the fabric side of the pieces show.

OBJECTIVES

1. To use cloth in a new way.

2. To capitalize on a child's natural interest as motivation.

3. To encourage children to discover ways of using cloth three-dimensionally.

4. To develop a sense of color and design in clothes.

5. To introduce clothing design as an art form.

(For Grades 1 through 6; adapted to K)

Lesson Five:

SPRING FEVER!

New Clothes

As soon as there are a few warm days, you know what happens—you get spring fever! And what's the first thing you want to do? Why, get some new clothes, of course! So let's give in to that feeling right now.

Collect as many different kinds of cloth as you can. You will need cloth that can be used for dresses, skirts, blouses, jumpers. You will need some for shirts, trousers, jackets, neckties. Yes, you'll need some for coats, too. You may even want something for new shoes or socks, or perhaps a scarf or just a new handkerchief.

That plaid cotton would make a pretty dress or a fine new sports shirt, wouldn't it? And think of the beautiful spring coat you could make from that bright wool. Can you find something for new trousers? Surely, that navy would be fine—perhaps that dark gray.

Continue to talk about the variety of materials and what each one suggests. Talk about the colors that look well together—the bright and dull colors, the light and dark ones. Talk about using prints and solid colors together. Let someone suggest material for a jumper and blouse, for a boy's slacks, for a party dress—for anything anyone would like to have.

But don't just talk about them too long. By now everyone will have determined what clothes he wants and what materials he will need for them. So let all the children take turns choosing one or two pieces of cloth. This will just be a beginning and they can get more as they need it.

If you're going to wear these clothes, you will have to become a lot smaller than you are now, so let's begin by making a little *you*! Then as you make the new clothes you will be able to model them!

Give out 12" x 18" manila or white drawing paper. Have each child make a picture of himself with crayons. Remember, only the head—and perhaps arms and legs—will show. So don't worry too much about the rest of it. You'll need shoulders for the dress or shirt or coat to rest on. And you'll need a small waistline for skirts or trousers.

When each person has sketched a person to wear the clothes he is going to make, let him cut it out. In the meantime you have given each person a little paste and he will be ready for the really interesting part— making a new outfit.

119

Are clothes just flat? No, a person isn't flat, so clothes can't be either. Can you think of any way of making them look a little bit three-dimensional, as though they really are on a person? Could you gather or pleat some part? Could you add a real pocket—one you could put a handkerchief in?

Encourage children—particularly the older ones—to add extra details that will complete the outfit. Perhaps the coat needs a collar. Would the dress look better with a scarf? Don't you need a belt for the slacks?

Making new spring clothes will be almost as much fun as buying them! You may even have designed some new styles! Certainly you'll want a fashion parade with each new outfit displayed on the bulletin board. Ah, spring fever!

Make It Easy—for Yourself!

1. Have the cloth torn or cut into individually sized pieces, about 6" x 9", before the class begins.
2. Spread the piles of cloth on a table or counter area so each kind of material can be seen. Let the children return to the supply area as often as they need to.
3. As you walk about the room during the lesson, collect the scraps of paper as the children finish making the paper figure. This will provide more work area for the children and will make the clean-up easier.
4. No pencils. Use crayons for the figure. Cut the cloth without previous drawing. Learn to "see" a shape without drawing it.

Variations

Make the kinds of clothes that other people wear. Younger children might make people they know: at home (mother, father); in the school (nurse, bus driver, custodian); in the community (policeman, fireman, grocer). Older children might create new clothing styles.

Variation for Lower Grades

Use paper instead of cloth for new clothes. Use colored construction paper for the plain "material" and gift wrapping or wallpaper for the printed "material."

O B J E C T I V E S

1. **To realize that art materials need not be limited to the usual crayon, paint, paper.**

2. **To introduce stitchery as a form of creative design.**

3. **To use line as the most important element of design.**

4. **To experiment with a new designing technique.**

(For Grades 4 through 6; adapted to Grades 2 and 3)

Lesson Six:

A STITCH IN TIME

Stitchery Designs

YOU'VE HEARD THE OLD ADAGE, "A STITCH IN time saves nine." These stitches will save much more than that—they will save whole, wonderful pictures.

Let's decide first what materials we'll need. This will be a fabric picture, so instead of paper we'll need cloth. Any kind of plain material will be fine. You may want an assortment of cloth to choose from: burlap, percale, monkscloth, smooth material or textured. Have a variety of colors, too—some dark, some light, some bright colors. Get a big assortment of yarns and threads—cotton roving, rug yarn, bulky knitting yarn, regular yarns, crewel and embroidery cotton, sewing thread—in a variety of colors. Then a large eye needle (crewel or tapestry) for each child and you will be all set to make your stitchery pictures.

You won't even have to know how to make any special stitches to make these designs. If you can thread a needle and sew a regular stitch, you can make lovely designs, for this time we're really just going to draw.

The first thing to do, then, is decide what you would like to draw. Will it be something realistic—a lovely tree, a graceful sailboat, a clown, an animal? Will it be a rural landscape, a city scene, a shoreline picture? Or will it be a nonobjective picture—geometric or freeform shapes, gentle-sweeping lines or twisting, jagged ones? You decide what you would like to make—or let the yarn and thread decide for you. Take a piece of yarn and drop it on the material. Is there the beginning of something real there? Move the yarn a bit—perhaps it will give you an idea. Change it several times—play with it a bit until you have an idea.

Change the color or the kind of yarn or thread, if you like, so that it fits your idea better. But now that you have a start, plan your lines carefully. If it is a sailboat you have decided to design, make that mast tall and straight.

There, that's fine, but how are you going to keep it there? If you had drawn it with crayon or paint, there wouldn't be any problem, would there? I suppose you could paste it to the cloth, but that would be just like when you use paper, wouldn't it? When you use cloth you . . . ? Sew, of course. So we'll thread a needle with fine yarn, embroidery cotton, or any other sewing "thread."

Now it will be easy to make that line stay just where we want it! How do you do that? Just start the needle from under the cloth (so that knot will be underneath), bring it up right alongside your line and down on the other side. Move the needle along a bit and repeat with another stitch right over your same line. Another space—another stitch; another space—another stitch. See how your line stays in place! It wouldn't have to be in a straight line, would it? You could draw a line with yarn just any place you wanted it to be—then tack it down with a stitch right on top of it.

Let everyone choose a piece of cloth and a beginning "line" color and a beginning "stitch" color. Take time to plan your picture. Perhaps you know just what you want it to be, so all you have to think of is the size, shape, and color. But perhaps you need to let the thread help you decide.

Move it around, change it, change it again. That's the way to do it! Take plenty of time to think and plan.

As you walk about the room, encourage the children to experiment before they begin to sew down the lines. Plan the large, important areas first; then you can add details later. Would a heavier yarn be good to use for the large part of your picture—or do you want all the lines to be the same thickness? Decide what you want your picture to look like, and then choose your materials carefully. Ask a question here, offer a bit of advice there; compliment, assist, help each child with his own particular problem.

Stitchery pictures take longer to make than pictures made with crayons or paint or even cut paper—but they are well worth it. Your class—and their teacher!—will be proud when their original designs are displayed. The old saying about a "stitch in time" will have new meaning.

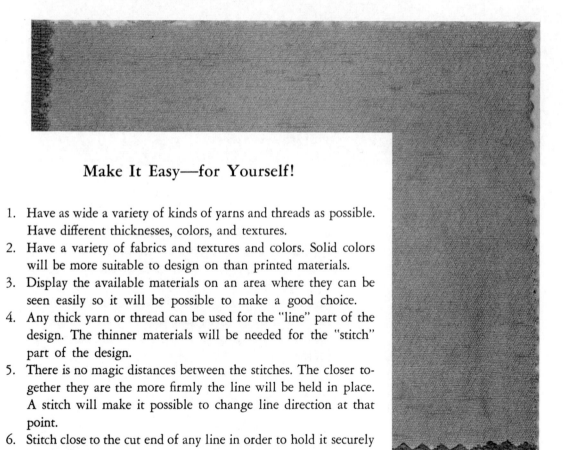

Make It Easy—for Yourself!

1. Have as wide a variety of kinds of yarns and threads as possible. Have different thicknesses, colors, and textures.
2. Have a variety of fabrics and textures and colors. Solid colors will be more suitable to design on than printed materials.
3. Display the available materials on an area where they can be seen easily so it will be possible to make a good choice.
4. Any thick yarn or thread can be used for the "line" part of the design. The thinner materials will be needed for the "stitch" part of the design.
5. There is no magic distances between the stitches. The closer together they are the more firmly the line will be held in place. A stitch will make it possible to change line direction at that point.
6. Stitch close to the cut end of any line in order to hold it securely in place.
7. Use the same color as the line to stitch with if you want to conceal the stitches; use a contrast in color if you want the stitches to form an important part of the design.

8. Take only one "line" color and one "stitch" color at a time. Come back to the sharing area for more whenever it is needed.
9. If this is the first stitchery experience, you may want to let your class experiment first. It will give them more confidence when they begin their own creations. Stitch a line to a small piece of fabric. Make it straight, make it curve, make it move in any direction. When they have the "feel" of the new technique, they can begin their designs.
10. Boys like to work with stitchery designs and do as well as the girls.

Variations

1. Use other techniques for designing on fabric—embroidery or applique or a combination of techniques. Have a variety of materials to be appliqued (plain or print, smooth or textured, lace, felt, tapestry).
2. Make a class mural. Plan it in the same way you would any mural, but use stitchery materials in place of paper and paint.
3. Make a wallhanging on which a few children work as a group project.

Variation for Lower Grades

Have the children make pictures of themselves or friends or family. Cut out the shapes and sew them to the background with yarn. Don't worry about rough edges. Emphasize the picture rather than the stitchery. You may have to thread the needles for them.

OBJECTIVES

1. To stimulate the use of painting for young people.

2. To enhance painting techniques through the use of an unusual background.

3. To create a contemporary look and a decorative effect in children's painting.

(For Grades 4 through 6; adopted to Grades K through 3)

Lesson Seven:

TAPESTRY 1–2–3!

Painting on Cloth

BORED WITH THE LOOK OF YOUR ROOM? Tired of the same old displays? Discouraged with the lack of artistic enthusiasm? Need a visual and mental lift? The solution is simple. How would you like some beautiful instant wall hangings to show the world? Yes, tapestry 1—2—3!

Don't be frightened, for these aren't really woven tapestries, but it's a great way to introduce painting on fabric. Children love the tales of King Arthur and his knights and will sit in awe as you tell about the large pictures made from cloth which adorned the castle walls—and about the wonderful banners with handsome emblems which hung on poles around the dining hall. With a simple question—"How would you like to make some wall hangings?"—you can have your class at its peak of artistic excitement.

Talk about what kind of designs or pictures could go on these hangings. Have the class suggest different motifs for their own pictures. Try to get them personally involved. For example, a favorite pet could be stylized with a spear or shield. Articles of clothing such as a treasured baseball cap, a hair bow, a ring, a glove, or an old shoe may also be turned into symbols of a new dynasty. Pictures such as seascapes, landscapes, people, or animals may also be considered for a tapestry. Banners may be made to proclaim a holiday, to stand as a class symbol, to be used in outdoor assemblies, to be used as stage decorations, or for a school gift from a departing class.

The technique is as simple as the possibilities are varied. All you need is poster paint and solid color material. Make sure the fabric has no wrinkles or creases. The fabric can be brought in by the class for individual hangings, or a couple of yards may be used for a larger tapestry done by the whole class. Burlap is an ideal fabric because of its rough texture and stiffness, but almost any other fabric may be used. If the only material available is too soft to handle or paint, it can be backed with construction paper. This is easily done by spreading paste over the paper and then placing the fabric over it. This is a good idea in any case, because when it's dry it can be cut into any shape without worrying about ragged edges.

Use charcoal, chalk, or crayons to sketch the picture or design on the fabric. Keep it simple without too many small details. Choose only a few colors of paint and apply to the sketch. If the paint is too thin or watery, powdered detergent may be added for body. The paint should be liquid enough to soak into the fibers but not so thin as to spread out of control. Paint the sketch in flat, broad areas for a dramatic look. Heavy outlines of black or contrasting colors may be also added, but this should be left up to the artist.

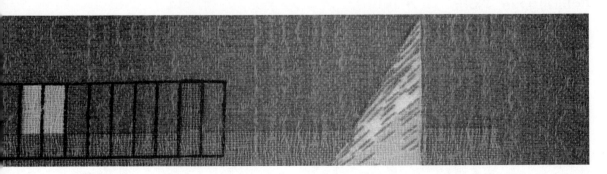

The banners or pictures may be hung on gold colored café curtain clips, or felt loops, or rope, or on dowels inserted in top and bottom hems. They can be highlighted with stitchery, cut into shield or triangular shapes, fringed or hemmed, or highlighted with bits of jewelry, buttons, or other fabrics. It's (1) easy to make, (2) fun to teach, (3) delightful to behold—tapestries 1—2—3!

Make It Easy—for Yourself!

1. Prepare the fabric before the picture is started. You can hem it, paste it to a paper backing, fringe it, or stretch it on a wooden frame.
2. Take a small swatch of fabric and test it with the paint to see if it takes the paint well.
3. Control the number of colors used by the class. Too many colors result in visual confusion. Three or four colors are enough.
4. Cover the desks, for in some cases the paint will go through the fabric.
5. Avoid sketching with pencils. This leads to small pictures which are impossible to paint.
6. Try to use interesting proportions of fabric. Use long and narrow pieces or cut them into arrow or shield shapes.

Variation for Lower Grades

Spread a large piece of burlap (or substitute) on a table. Have each child stand around it holding a container of paint and a brush. Using one theme, have each child paint an outline of the chosen subject (birds, flowers, fish). After they all have completed one object, they turn and take five steps, stop, and paint another object. This is continued until the entire canvas is filled with outlined objects. Next, go around the table yourself with a container of white paint. Add a little white to each child's paint, making it a pastel. Have the class repeat the ring-around-the-table routine, but this time they paint in the outlined shapes. You may have them use the same color to fill in, or another color. You may have them paint in their own shape or any shape they choose. Since some of the drawings are upside down in this kind of mural, choose a subject which can stand by itself—such as blossoms, fish, flying birds, or freeform shapes.

O B J E C T I V E S

1. To use crayons in a new way—with a new material.

2. To allow each person to contribute to a group project.

3. To provide opportunity for using individual ideas related to a group theme.

(For Grades 1 through 6; adapted to K)

Lesson Eight:

THAT'S WHAT'S DIFFERENT!

Crayon on Cloth

YOU ASK, WHAT'S DIFFERENT ABOUT USING crayons? Nothing, nothing at all—if you use them on paper. But when you use crayons on cloth—well, that's what's different!

You won't need any other materials, either—just cloth and crayons. What kind of cloth? Why any plain material—unbleached muslin or just an old sheet, white or any light color. Tear the sheet into pieces about ten inches square so that each child will have one square on which he can draw his picture.

That's just about all there is to it, for you can draw just as well on cloth as you can on paper. Oh, the cloth moves around a little bit, so you'll have to hold on to it more than if it were paper. But that isn't much of a problem, is it?

Decide what you would like your crayon on cloth drawings to be about. This time they should all be about the same subject because we're going to sew all the pieces together when we have them finished—like a big wall hanging, or a very special table cover, or a drape to enclose an open cupboard, or—well, anything you'd like to use such a pretty thing for. Perhaps you'll have an underwater theme—with fat round fish and long skinny ones and flying ones, with seaweed and rocks and sand, with an octopus and a seahorse and snail or two. Or choose any subject you would like: spring, with gay butterflies and birds and flowers and even a few bugs; sports, with skaters and baseball players, football goals, and gay banners.

After you have chosen the subject, talk about it for a while with your class. Talk about all the different things that could go into it. Would they all look the same? Certainly not! What would they be doing? What shapes would· they be? What colors? Get as many different individual ideas as you can. Then pass out the crayons and go to work.

These pictures will all be sewn together, so don't let your picture go too close to the edge. Some of the edge of the square will be used in the seam, you know. Press quite hard on the crayon—not so hard that you leave a thick layer of wax, just hard enough to make good, bright colors. That's the way to do it! Fill in the things you have drawn, just as you would do if you had drawn them on paper. Don't fill in the whole background, of course. Leave that just the white (or tinted) cloth.

Urge the class to use lots of color as the colors will be slightly dulled when the cloth pieces are ironed. Oh, yes, the crayon-on-cloth pictures should be ironed when they are finished. This makes the color on the cloth permanent so that the finished piece may even be laundered.

As individual children complete their pictures, let them bring them to the ironing area and gently press them. Lay them face down on the newspaper, put another piece of newspaper over them, and press them with a moderately hot iron. See what has happened! The color has gone all the way through the cloth. There it is, on the back of your picture! How do you suppose that happened? That's right! The heat from the iron melted the wax in the crayon and went right through the cloth. So of course the color had to go through, too!

Explain why that is important—why crayon pictures should be ironed and paper ones don't have to be. Cloth gets dirty and has to be laundered, doesn't it? There wouldn't be much point to making a picture on cloth if the color all washed out!

Once all the ironing has been completed the pictures will be finished. Have a quick showing. Point out all the individual ideas you talked about earlier, the variety, the new ways people have found to do a thing. Then collect them all and tuck them out of sight until you have time to sew them all together. (Find a helpful friend if you don't sew.)

All of you will be surprised when you see the completed hanging, or table cover, or whatever you decided it should be. The one big picture will look even better than all the separate ones did.

Make It Easy—for Yourself!

1. Tear the cloth so that all the pieces are square and exactly the same size. This is important so that when they are sewn together each picture will fit next to any other picture.
2. Use only wax crayons. In order for the color to become permanent on the cloth, the *wax* must melt and carry the color with it.
3. Have as much variety in color as possible. If possible, use boxes of crayons that have at least twenty-four colors.
4. Press reasonably hard when applying the crayons. If only a thin layer of color is used, there will be neither enough color or wax to penetrate the cloth. Don't go to the other extreme, however,

and apply crayon so heavily that it leaves a thick coating of wax. This would have too much wax to go through the cloth and so the surplus wax would spread—with the color—into adjoining areas. The right amount is just a normally heavy use of the crayon.

5. Prepare an ironing area by making a thick pad of newspaper. Several sections of newspaper will assure that the heat from the iron does not penetrate to the underneath surface. Have several additional pieces of newspaper so that occasionally a fresh piece can be put on top of the picture to be ironed.

6. Before sewing the pieces together arrange all of them so that they create an interesting over-all effect. Then sew them together in strips and, last of all, sew the strips together into a whole. If the blocks do not come out evenly, add plain squares to the edges—or use one or more blocks for a title—with crayon.

7. The ironed pictures are washable. Of course, launder them carefully by hand.

8. No pencils! Draw with the crayons.

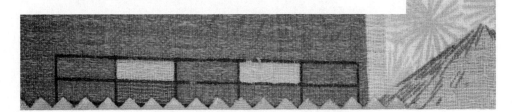

Variations

1. Make completely individual pictures—not to be sewn together. These might be somewhat larger, perhaps about 12″ x 18″. They might be made as regular pictures or used as placemats. They would not need to be related to a class theme.

2. Make a large class picture just as you would any mural.

3. Make individual—or group—pictures using a combination of wax crayons and stitchery.

Variation for Lower Grade

Make individual drawings on cloth: Myself; The Toy I Like Best; My Best Friend.

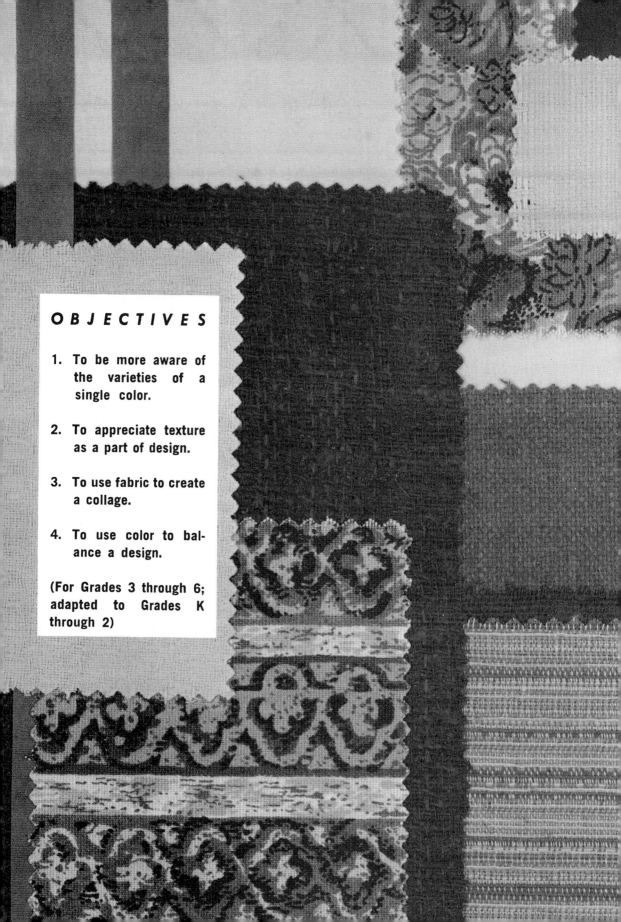

OBJECTIVES

1. To be more aware of the varieties of a single color.

2. To appreciate texture as a part of design.

3. To use fabric to create a collage.

4. To use color to balance a design.

(For Grades 3 through 6; adapted to Grades K through 2)

Lesson Nine:

CLOTH IS FOR PASTING

Cloth Color Collage

PERHAPS YOU'VE MADE A DRESS OR SOME living room drapes. You sewed them, and then there were some scraps left over. You were going to throw those scraps away—after all, they were just little pieces, not big enough for anything else. But wait a minute! Cloth is for pasting, too—and hardly anything is too small for that.

You'll be surprised how many scraps of cloth you can save in a short time—left over pieces from the skirt or dress you made; the old housecoat you were going to throw away; the piece you cut off the gown you shortened. Your neighbors will probably be willing to add to your collection. Perhaps you know a dressmaker or someone who sells materials and will be able to boost your supply of odds and ends. Children in your class will enjoy seeing the increase in variety as they make their contributions, too. Before long you will have a big box full of fabric—print materials and plain, textured fabrics and shiny smooth ones, endless shades of blue and green, red and yellow, purple and brown, black and white.

Motivation for the lesson has increased with each new addition to the box of materials. Now all you have to do is make use of it. Cut off enough tiny pieces of solid color material so that there is one for each child in your class. Have at least one of every color and several pieces of those colors that you have the most of. Put all those little pieces in a small box. As you carry it to each child in your class, let him reach in and take one. No peeking, now—just take any one.

What do you suppose these little pieces of material are for? Yes, I suppose you could use them in your collage—the kind of picture you are going to make, but you will need lots more cloth than that, won't you? Your fabric collage—or cloth pasting—will fill the whole paper, not just a little spot like this. So can you think of another reason for that tiny piece of cloth you chose? What you really chose was a . . . ? Right, a color! Whatever color you have will be the color of your collage.

Let's see how that will be. Your color is blue, so everything you put in

133

your collage must be blue. Go to the box of fabric and spread out the scraps on the table. Find several pieces of blue material—dark blue, light blue, bright blue, grey blue, green blue, just several kinds of the one color. Look how many kinds there are! And besides being different kinds of blue, they feel different. They are different textures—and that makes them look different, too! So you will have lots of variety for your blue collage. There is something else that is blue, too. Yes, look at this lovely piece of printed material. Oh, there are some other colors on it—that's what makes it a print. But it is mostly blue, isn't it? So that could be part of your collage, too.

Have some small pieces of manila drawing paper to paste the cloth to. These color collages are to be made entirely of fabric, so none of the paper will show. Do you think you should begin with little pieces of cloth or big pieces? Certainly—use large pieces first to cover all of the background. Then you can paste smaller pieces over the larger ones if you like. You could even add several layers of cloth, overlapping them any way that looks good.

Talk about balance in the design—using the same kind of fabric in different parts of the collage, smaller areas of dark or bright colors to balance larger areas of light or dull colors, groups of small shapes to balance a larger shape.

Let a few children at a time come to the fabric area and choose several pieces of material of their color. As this is being done, pass out newspaper for pasting, manila paper to paste the collage to, paste, paste brushes, and scissors. Then everyone to work!

Do you think you should try to fit the edges of shapes together? Or would it be better to overlap the big shapes? Right—it would be pretty hard to fit shapes into each other, but it would be easy to overlap them to cover all the paper. So cover the whole paper first with large pieces of cloth. Make them simple shapes—it will be easy to add other things later.

Oh, don't worry about the edges of the paper. Let the cloth go right off all the edges. It will be easy to make them even later on.

Continue to question, suggest, encourage as you go from one child to another. Warn one not to use too many kinds of print materials. One or two kinds of prints add interest; too many prints make the design confusing. Compliment another on his repetiton of line. That helps to create rhythm in the collage. Ask another child what he can do to balance a big, plain area. Several things could be done—several small shapes, a print, a brighter variety of his color. Try out several, then choose the one that you like best.

All at once the design will come to life and the collage will be just about finished. Perhaps it will need just one more piece of cloth where it will attract special attention. Perhaps two parts of the collage should be connected so that your eye moves easily from one to another. Perhaps it needs—well, you look at it and see if it needs anything else. But when it is just right don't add one extra thing!

If you have a paper cutter, you will find it more satisfactory to trim the edges yourself than to have each child do it with his scissors. Have a quick showing—you'll be delighted with them! The children may even give them names. Then mount them on a plain paper background before having a more permanent exhibition.

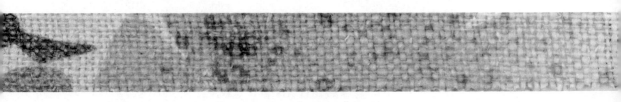

Make It Easy—for Yourself!

1. Talk about the meaning of "collage." It comes from a French word meaning "pasting." So a collage is just a picture which has been pasted together.
2. Have several sizes and shapes of manila paper for the back of the collage: pieces about seven or eight inches square, long narrow pieces about four by ten inches, or an in-between size.
3. No pencils! Cut the shapes without any preliminary drawing.
4. If possible, have a pair or two of pinking shears available. It is a simple way of adding a touch of interest.
5. Urge children to use only one or two kinds of prints in their collages. Too many kinds would make the collage "busy."
6. The edges of the collage will be neater and more even if they are trimmed on a paper cutter than if they are cut by hand with a pair of scissors.
7. Mount the finished collages on white drawing paper for background. Light collages—white and yellow—will need a narrow edging of a darker color before mounting on the white paper.
8. Do all the pasting on newspaper to keep the collage clean. If you do not have paste brushes, make an applicator from any scrap paper. Fold a small piece of paper over several times and then bend it in the middle.
9. Clean up the easy way. Collect the scissors and paste brushes. Fold all the scraps (cloth, paste paper, and paste applicators if they were used) inside the newspaper. Have one or two people collect the folded newspaper and put it in the wastebasket.

Variations

1. Make a similar fabric collage but use any pleasing color combinations.
2. Make a one-color collage using a variety of materials besides cloth—construction paper, corrugated paper, yarn, cotton roving, buttons.
3. Plan a costume. Make all of the person and the costume from cloth.

Variations for Lower Grades

1. Make a picture of something real. Use only cloth or make the main part of the picture from fabric and complete it with paint or crayons.
2. Make any kind of picture. Use fabric for anything in the picture which would normally be made of cloth.

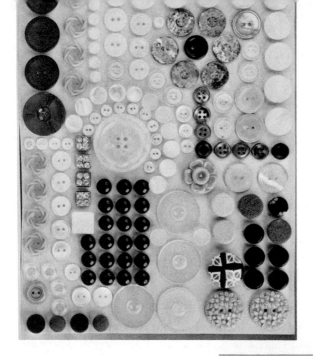

OBJECTIVES

1. To use common household items in a novel way.

2. To create a pleasing pattern from one basic shape.

3. To create rhythm and balance through repetition.

(For Grades 4 through 6)

Lesson Ten:

BUTTON, BUTTON–
WHO'S GOT THE BUTTON?

Button Mosaics

IT MAY HAVE BEEN A LONG TIME SINCE YOU
have played the game of "Button, button, who's got the button?" But you'll
ask that question all over again as you work on your button mosaic.

137

What is a mosaic, anyway? Talk about it with your class. Perhaps there is a mosaic wall at a nearby supermarket, or in the lobby of an office building—or perhaps even in your school. You may have made a mosaic before out of paper or linoleum. In any case, you find that a mosaic is a picture made of small pieces that have been put together with a little space left between the parts. Mosaics can be pictures of anything—they can be made of anything. Perhaps someone would like to look up more information about mosaics.

But enough of that for now. Let's make our own mosaics, a kind you've never seen before—button mosaics! Have your class gathered around you, and as you begin to talk, take a jar full of all kinds of buttons and spread them out on a table. I'll bet you didn't know there were so many kinds of buttons! Look at them! All kinds of colors and sizes! They aren't all round, either, are they? Just enjoy them for a minute or two. Find the largest button, the smallest one, the fattest one. And look, there's a square one! Yes, there's a strange one—looks like a bug, doesn't it? You're right! There are two buttons that are exactly alike. And there's another one just like them. Let's put them together.

As you find different kinds of buttons push them to one side. Begin to move them about to create an interesting pattern. If this were going to be my mosaic, I would need to put them on a heavy paper for the background and then fill in the empty spaces, wouldn't I? Well, let's do that. There are many more gray buttons than any other color, so perhaps I should plan to make most of my mosaic gray and use other colors just for contrast.

Talk about the things that make a good design. Find a variety of buttons—different sizes, different colors, different shapes. But don't get too much variety, for there have to be similar things in a good design, too. So perhaps we should eliminate a few of the things that are different and find some buttons that are like others we already have.

Do you think we should put these five buttons that are just alike all together, or should they be in five different places? Well, that's hard to say, isn't it? Let's look and see what we could do with them. Put them all together as a group—they almost make a solid area, don't they? Put them in five different parts of your design and they become five separate spots, don't they? Or put them in a line, a straight line or a curved line—and they make your eye move along that line. So you will have to decide what you want them to do in your picture. Then, when your mosaic is planned just the way you want it, all you have to do is glue all the parts to the background. How can you do that without changing your arrangement? That's easy enough—just pick up one button at a time, put a spot of glue on the back of it, and replace it.

When everyone is back at his own desk, pass out the necessary materials—newspaper to cover the desks, heavy cardboard on which to arrange the mosaic, a big variety of buttons to share, and, of course, glue.

Look over your collection of buttons and decide what color you have enough of to make an important part of your mosaic. Begin to arrange them into an interesting pattern. Oh, don't be afraid to move them about—maybe you will like them better in another place.

As the work progresses some children may need special buttons to complete their designs. Someone may ask, "Button, button, who has a blue button?" or red? or yellow? or whatever the case may be. When at last every button has been glued into its proper place, gather all the leftover buttons and put them away to use another day.

Make It Easy—for Yourself!

1. Arrange desks in groups of four or six. Have one desk as a sharing desk for the three or five children in the group. Spread the buttons out on the extra desk for anyone in the group to use. This will allow a wider and better choice than if each child had his own limited supply.
2. Cover all desks with newspaper to protect their surfaces from the glue.
3. Use a quick drying glue. Paste will not adhere to buttons.
4. No pencils! Move the buttons about and let them determine what form the mosaic will take.
5. Leave only tiny spaces between the buttons so that the areas of color look solid rather than spotted.
6. As the mosaics become almost finished, let the children share with other groups to find just the right buttons.
7. Glue takes longer than paste to set, so let the mosaics dry thoroughly before moving them much.

Variations

1. Use the buttons as part of a collage. Make the main part of the collage of paper or fabric. Use the buttons for accents or to cover some areas.
2. Make a mosaic from bits of jewelry, rickrack, or other trimming. Make it realistic or non-objective.

from the

BATHROOM
LAUNDRY

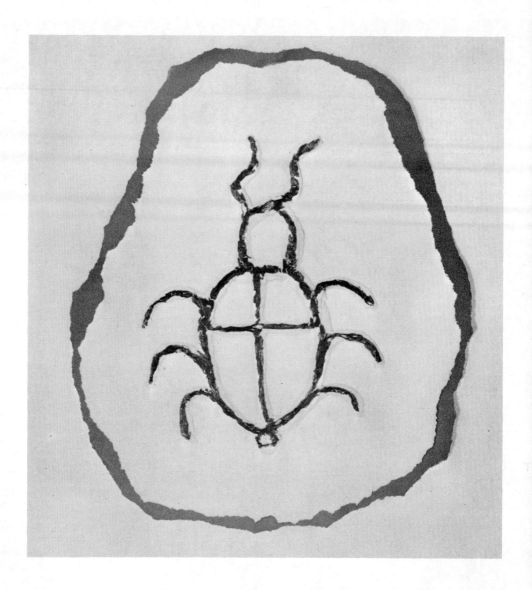

OBJECTIVES

1. To use a common household material to make a semi three-dimensional picture.

2. To learn to use lines to create a well designed picture.

3. To use lines to create areas.

(For Grades 3 through 6)

Lesson One:

STRINGLESS STRING

Papier-Mâché Pictures

WE WON'T NEED ANY STRING FOR THIS
—not regular string, at least. Instead we'll use stringless string! Never
heard of it? Well, we'll make it. We'll make it out of face tissue—or toilet
tissue. And then we'll use our stringless string to make all kinds of wonderful things.

Prepare all your materials ahead of time. You will need enough newspaper to thoroughly cover all the work areas. Prepare, also, the papier-
mâché materials: a pile of face tissue and a supply of soft, rather thin wheat
paste for each group of children. Distribute the wheat paste on paper plates.
This provides easy to use and easy to dispose of containers. Each person will
also need a piece of 12″ x 18″ white or colored construction paper for the
background of the picture.

Now that we have all these materials together, what are you going to
do with them? Well, you can make a dog or a dinosaur, an elf or an elephant, a bug or a bugle, a man or a mouse, a . . . or a . . . . You decide
what you are going to make—anything that has a distinctive outline that
you can recognize.

Let me see. I think I will make . . . a bug! But first I have to make a
piece of stringless string. I'll do that by taking a piece of this face tissue,
holding it vertically over my work area. I'll dip the fingers of my other hand
into that soft, gooey paste. Like that. Run your fingers down the tissue. Dip
your fingers in the paste again and a second time move them down the
tissue. Perhaps this time you will want to hold the tissue from the bottom
end so that the paste will be distributed more evenly. See—it doesn't look
like a face tissue anymore, does it? It is becoming long and thin—like a
string! Continue to run it through your fingers until all the edges are packed
tightly together—until it is just a line.

What do you ever do with a line? Why, of course—you draw with it!
So I will begin to draw my bug. Lay one end of the papier-mâché string
on the paper and let the line move in an oval shape as you gradually lay

it on the paper. It didn't go very far, did it—not for a big bug. Well, that's no problem. Just make another line.

Repeat the process of making another papier-mâché string. Then attach it to the one that is already on your paper. Overlap the ends—about an inch or so. That will make it stronger, so that when my bug is dry it won't fall apart. Continue making more papier-mâché strings until the bug is finished. Add a head, several rounding lines for legs, antennae coming from the head. Each time a line is added, be sure it overlaps the preceding line. Press the edges together by rubbing your fingers firmly against each side of the papier-mâché. Add some lines to the inside of your bug to make it more interesting.

There—that looks like a pretty special bug. You wouldn't mind having him around, would you?

Have some tempera paint and an easel brush handy. Lightly color the top edge of all the ridges that make up your bug. This will make the design show even better.

Place the finished design where it can dry. Sun or other direct heat will not make it crack. The background paper will warp as the papier-mâché dries (as will any paper that has been wet), but this will not harm the finished picture. When the papier-mâché is dry, you may want to cut a freeform shape around the object or cut around the picture, leaving a border of about one inch.

As the children finish their pictures, let them wipe the excess paste from their hands with a paper towel. Have them put the paper towel and any scraps of left over tissue on the paper plate of paste which can be wrapped in the newspaper.

You will never recognize the face tissue that made the stringless string —but you will enjoy every creature it made.

Make It Easy—for Yourself!

1. Cover all work areas with newspaper.
2. Mix the wheat paste in a large can or paper container that can be discarded.
3. Distribute wheat paste on paper plates so that they can be thrown away. They simplify the problem of clean-up. They also provide an easy access to the paste.
4. Push four to six desks together to make one work area. One desk should be left as a supply area—with a paper plate of paste and a pile of tissue. One child could work at each of the other three to five desks.
5. It will be easier if the children stand to work.
6. Use *every* scrap of tissue before getting another piece. (Even tiny pieces that pull off the "string" can be added to the design to strengthen it.)
7. Hold the tissue over the work area so that if any paste drops it will fall on the newspaper.
8. If you use toilet tissue, rip it into uneven numbers of sections (about seven) and fold it in half. This will strengthen the perforated areas and prevent them from tearing apart.
9. Give each child a paper towel so that he can wipe most of the paste off his hands when he has finished. This will prevent the need for any rush to wash hands.
10. The tissue string picture may be painted while it is still wet. Paint only the top edge to give a touch of color.
11. No pencils! Draw with the tissue string.

Variations

1. Make freeform shapes instead of real things. Be sure the lines cross over each other to add both interest and strength.
2. Make a simplified scene or still life.
3. Use other materials for similar pictures: paper napkins, colored tissue paper.
4. Make the objects on wax paper. When the papier-mâché is dry, carefully remove the wax paper. Colored tissue paper or cellophane may be glued to the back of some open areas.

OBJECTIVES

1. To present a simple craft project in the classroom.

2. To present a simple lesson with a chance for individual differences and personal creativity.

3. To construct three-dimensional flowers to be used as decoration in the home or classroom.

(For Grades 4 through 6)

Lesson Two:

OLÉ, OLÉ!

Toilet Tissue Flowers

MEXICAN CRAFTSMEN MAKE THE MOST unique and beautiful flowers from crepe paper. Using the same technique, you can create luscious blooms that will enhance your room and make you want to shout, "Olé! Olé!"

The technique is simple, so your students will be assured of success and filled with pride as they assume the role of an old Mexican craftsman. All that is needed is a long, long length of toilet tissue, some paste, a pipe cleaner or stick, and perhaps some string.

Take a long strip of tissue (twice your height is good) and start folding it on the perforated lines so that you end up with a flat roll. Now we shape our petals according to our own design. The principle of cutting out half a shape on a fold to obtain a whole object (such as in a heart for a valentine) can be used here. The flat roll has two folds, one on each side and has loose edges on the top and bottom.

Start on the fold side and cut from the top down, forming half a petal. Continue cutting back up to the center of the loose edge, then down again to form a whole petal shape. Cut up to the top of the other folded side forming another half petal. The result should look like an uneven scallop, that is, half a petal, a whole petal, and a half petal. When unrolled you have a continuous line of petals approximately the same size and shape.

Remember, the size and shape of the petals are up to the artist. They can be rounded, pointed, floppy, stiff, torn instead of cut, or can be interpreted in many other ways. Instead of cutting one petal with two halves, more or fewer petals can be cut. The only thing which must remain constant is that the fold must be left intact—or the flower will fall apart.

Forming the blossom is a simple matter, but precautions must be taken. When the flat roll is unfurled and placed flat on a desk, paste is applied to the uncut edge for about a foot at a time. Gather (bunch up) the pasted edge the length of one square of tissue, then place a pipe cleaner or stick on top of it. Gather the next square and roll the stick over it. Apply more paste, gather the edge, and roll the stick. This is done until the entire length is rolled. Be careful to roll over the previously gathered edges and not travel down the stick. Roll slowly and carefully so that the overlapping petals form a lush and full blossom. If the tissue is not gathered enough or if the petals are not cut deep enough the flower will be stiff and straight.

When the length of tissue is completely rolled, string or tape may be wrapped around the base of the flower for good support. Gently open the blossom, pulling down each layer of petals so that the flower is full and graceful. If the length of tissue tears or part of it becomes unworkable and must be eliminated, simply take the unused part and continue as if it were a whole piece.

When these flowers are made from pastel tissue or printed tissue—as well as with white—they are delightful to behold and will add beauty and softness to any display. It's all over but the shouting—olé, that is.

Make It Easy—for Yourself!

1. Control the length of tissue being used by the students. Too long a piece will not allow for easy cutting and too short a piece will result in a skimpy bloom.
2. When the petals are cut, place the roll flat on the desk and open it away from you, exposing only a few petals at a time.
3. Don't roll down the stick—each rolling must go over the one before.
4. Gather the tissue tightly, making sure it is stuck together.
5. Cut the petals at least three-quarters down the width of the tissue, but be careful not to go too near the edge. This would make it too fragile to handle.
6. Wrap the string or tape tightly over the base of the blossom, covering part of the stick, also. This will make a more graceful base.

Variations

1. Use crepe paper already in flat rolls to make giant size blossoms. A strip at the top of the roll can be cut off and used to make a rolled center around which the larger petals (of another color) are formed.
2. Use colored tissue and make flowers of any size. More than one color can be used for a multi-color blossom. This is easy to achieve by starting with a strip of one color and continuing with strips of other colors.

OBJECTIVES

1. To create fun-filled mobiles from discarded cardboard tubes.

2. To discover an easy way of making marionettes.

3. To use familiar forms to stimulate imaginations.

(For Grades 4 through 6; adapted to Grades 1 through 3)

Lesson Three:

SQUIGGLY, WIGGLY, JIGGLY

Cardboard Tube Constructions

HAVE YOU LOOKED AROUND your classroom lately? Notice how static everything is? Want to add some movement? Some excitement? Something different? How about something squiggly, wiggly, and jiggly?

You don't need a lot of art materials for this project—in fact all you need are some cardboard tubes from inside of toilet tissue rolls, paper towel rolls, mailing tubes, or any rolled papers. Just looking at these tubes might suggest arms, legs, and bodies of people or animals. That's pretty obvious—but how to go about making them into creative creatures? That's the question. This can be done painlessly with a little masking tape and a lot of imagination.

Accumulate a variety of tubes—long, short, wide, narrow—lots and lots of them. Bring in a roll of narrow masking tape, or have the students make their own. This is easily done by cutting small rectangles of cloth and putting paste on one side when needed. (Paper is not really strong enough for this lesson, but it may be adequate if fabric is not available.) All we have to do is combine these tubes to create many different effects.

How about making some imaginary people? That's fun and easy, too! We can take three long tubes of the same size, lay them one next to the other, and wrap our tape around them—or just glue them together. Presto—the broad chest of a soldier or a clown ready for the rest of his costume.

To make a leg, take a tube and insert a piece of tape into the top of it, and continue the end of it into the outer tube. Leave a small space between the tubes to allow for movement. Do this again on the other tube to make the other leg. Attach his arms with tape in a similar manner so that they will be floppy, too. His head can be cut from a tube and taped on sideways. This also works for feet, hats, or ears.

Hold the tube in a horizontal position to make the body of an animal. One tube equals a skinny body while two or three make a stocky creature.

151

Tape all the appendages on loosely so that there is a lot of movement. The people and creatures won't stand up alone. They're not meant to. We must add some strings to give them life.

If your creature is meant to be suspended as a mobile, one string may be enough. He gets his movement from air currents. If you want your creature to walk or dance, more strings are necessary. One string to support his body and additional strings to arms and legs will make your marionette come to life. Attach all these strings to a stick which may be held in one hand while the marionette is directed by the other hand.

Bright colors can be added with paint or colored paper or scrap materials brought in from home. Costumes and facial expressions are important to build an interesting character.

Hours of fun can be had in and out of school from these marvelous creatures. You, too, will be tempted to make them wiggle, jiggle, and squiggle!

Make It Easy—for Yourself!

1. Have the class bring in a lot of tubes over a period of time to insure that there are enough at art time.
2. Cover the desks when glue is used so that it will not harm the finish.
3. Have the children think of characters with which they are familiar.
4. Details of dress and features can be pasted directly onto the creature. Tape is necessary for movement.
5. String may be substituted for tape, but it becomes more involved and is more difficult to use.
6. Encourage the use of many scrap materials such as yarn, cotton roving, buttons, and jewelry.
7. Use a strong glue, especially where weight and movement are important.

Variation

Use a long tube as the beginning of a mobile. Cut slits into the tube, add knotted string, and attach other tubes. Balance the tubes so that the mobile swings and moves gently. Strings may be attached at the ends or through the middle of the tubes. Try to get good balance and movement with a variety of tubes.

Variation for Lower Grades

Use a tube as the basic form and add cut paper legs, arms, head, and anything else needed to complete a figure. Tie or tape one string from the top of the tube and either suspend it or hold it for movement. The arms and legs can be made from accordion folded strips of paper for a bouncier marionette.

OBJECTIVES

1. To introduce abstract sculpture to children.

2. To utilize pre-determined shapes in a creative three-dimensional form.

3. To use found, familiar materials for an art lesson.

4. To create balance and rhythm with one basic shape.

(For Grades 4 through 6)

Lesson Four:

THE AGE OF THE AEROSOL

Bottle Top Sculpture

THIS IS TRULY THE AGE OF THE AEROSOL spray can. There are sprays to attract and sprays to repel, sprays to change a color, sprays to hold a hairdo, sprays to shave with, sprays to clear the air, and even sprays to just spray! They come in all sizes—small, family, jumbo, and king size. They come in different shapes and even in decorator designs. They're handy to use, expensive to buy, and a shame to throw away.

Let's save at least the tops and see what we can do with them in a creative way. Let's make a modern fantastic sculpture with them.

We'll need a few other things, too. We'll need cement (model type) and some stiff cardboard such as comes with new shirts or from the backs of writing pads. In order to add a little more variety, let's add some unusual bottle caps to our collection. We don't want too many of the common soda bottle caps; instead we want the new and different kinds found on many commercial products such as mouthwash, shampoos, toothpaste, after-shave lotion, and colognes. Some of these are in color, others come in a softer translucent plastic, or some are made of shiny metal. We want variety. Search the house and you'll be amazed by the variety of tops you'll find.

How do we get started? First take a collection of tops and caps and see how they relate to one another. Perhaps you can find a large cap and contrast it with a small top, or maybe the bright colored top will look good with that small white one. Cut a piece of cardboard a few inches larger than the cap and cement them together. Leave part of the cardboard extended beyond the cap to make a little shelf on which other caps may be placed. Your construction will now start to grow as you add more caps, tops, and cardboard in different height layers and in different directions. You may want to cement top on top or perhaps you'd prefer a layer of cardboard between each top. You can also use the cardboard as a bridge between different areas of the construction. There are no set rules as to how to build your sculpture. It's all a matter of what you're trying to show or say.

Your sculpture can be low and spread out or tall and majestic, simple or complex. Try to look at it from all directions while you're working on

155

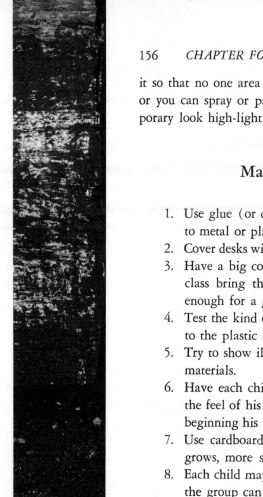

it so that no one area is left unfinished. The sculpture can remain as it is, or you can spray or paint it. The effect is one of a dramatic and contemporary look high-lighting the fact that this truly is the age of the aerosol.

Make It Easy—for Yourself!

1. Use glue (or cement) rather than paste. Paste will not adhere to metal or plastic.
2. Cover desks with newspaper to protect the surface from the glue.
3. Have a big collection of spray tops and bottle tops. Have the class bring them in over a period of time to insure having enough for a good sized sculpture from each child.
4. Test the kind of cement to be used to make sure it will adhere to the plastic or metal tops.
5. Try to show illustrations of modern sculpture done in unusual materials.
6. Have each child work for a few minutes without glue to get the feel of his materials and to discover several possibilities for beginning his work.
7. Use cardboard which is stiff and strong because, as the piece grows, more strain will be placed on the board.
8. Each child may have his own collection of tops, or a supply for the group can be spread over a table from which the students select a few items at a time.
9. Try to stress the need for variety, both in the collection of supplies and in the actual sculpture. Avoid flat, fence-like constructions.

Variations

1. Small sculptures made by the class may be put together to make a large construction for the classroom.
2. Small individual constructions may be used as part of a large mobile, or each child can make his own mobile from his little construction.
3. Make a semi three-dimensional rhythm and line composition by gluing or nailing the tops to an interesting background such as wood, cork, or plastic. Tops may be adhered upside down or rightside up to add variety to the finished composition.

O B J E C T I V E S

1. To introduce a new kind of painting in the schoolroom.

2. To introduce the basic feel of oil painting to children.

3. To satisfy the need for variation in painting techniques for older children.

(For Grades 4 through 6)

Lesson Five:

GO, GO, VAN GOGH

Detergent Painting

"GO, GO, VAN GOGH" MAY BECOME THE WAR chant of your class after one of the most exciting and rewarding art lessons you can present. The beauty of this lesson is found in its simplicity both

157

for the student and for the teacher. Imagine having the beauty of an oil painting right in the classroom!

Let's go back to Van Gogh for a moment and take a look at one of his paintings. Almost any one will do as long as it shows how the paint was used to create depth and texture and movement. Notice how emotional each brush stroke is, how much actual thick paint can be seen even in a print of the painting. Wouldn't it be great if we could achieve this kind of oil painting in school? We can! and we don't have to invest any money in expensive oil sets. All we need is regular school poster paints, brushes, and a box of regular washday powdered detergent.

As you know, there are certain limitations to using poster (tempera) paints. You must be careful not to get one wet color next to another or it will run. We cannot overlap wet colors for the same reason. Neither can we build up thick layers of paint or effectively show brush strokes. Tempera paint is good in itself and produces effects which can't be done as well with other types of paints, but let's get a little variety in our art program and break away from strict tempera painting.

Get four coffee cans with plastic tops and pour a jar of paint into each one. Use the primary colors—red, yellow, and blue—plus white. Slowly pour and stir in the powdered detergent until the paint takes on the consistency of whipped cream. The amount of detergent that will be used varies with each color and brand of paint. You can prepare the paint the day before as long as you keep it tightly covered. If it becomes too thick or dry, more paint or water can be added.

Give each child a papier-mâché egg carton, or half of one, or a paper plate, or a piece of cardboard, or a piece of paper, or anything flat which can be used as a palette. In each can of paint place a tongue depressor or

spoon with which the paint can be scooped onto the palette. Have each child come to the coffee cans and take a small amount of paint on his palette. He may come back again when he needs more paint.

Instead of a piece of canvas for our background, construction paper or cardboard can be used. The stronger it is the better. The picture may be sketched on this background with charcoal or chalk, but this should be done freely without details. New colors like orange, green, purple, brown, and the pastel tints, may be mixed on the palette or on the picture.

We can now start to paint freely. We can blend colors, overlap colors, and streak colors. We can show brush strokes, build up thick areas, and use a dry brush. It is easy now to paint the entire paper, including the background, for a more finished look. The paint dries very quickly which also helps in making it easier to use. Have a pail of water so that anyone may wash his brush if he so desires before using another color.

When the painting has dried thoroughly it may take on a white powdery appearance. This can be eliminated with a coat of varnish. A varnished picture really looks like an oil painting. When you think of your original inspiration you, too, may shout "Go, go, Van Gogh!"

Make It Easy—for Yourself!

1. Prepare the paint in advance and make sure it is not too thick.
2. After the picture has been sketched, start painting the background first. This will make the subject of your painting more sharp and important.
3. In a central location have a pail half full of water. Don't have too much water in it because as the brushes are washed thick soap suds form.
4. Give each child a stiff brush—such as a half inch easel brush.
5. Caution the children not to try to put too many details in their pictures. Much of it will be lost because of the thickness of the paint.

from the

ATTIC
GARAGE
CELLAR

OBJECTIVES

1. To create non-objective design from scrap wood and nails.

2. To add personal meaning to abstract design.

3. To introduce design in a unique way.

4. To provide opportunity for a more manual use of art materials.

(For Grades 5 and 6)

Lesson One:

DESIGNS WITH A BANG!

Nail Designs on Wood

YOU'VE MADE DESIGNS WITH PAPER, paint, and crayon which have been interesting—and quiet. How about doing some designs with a three-dimensional look—designs with a polished look—designs with a different look—designs with a bang! You can create contemporary pieces that will be unique and exciting and all you need are wood, nails, and a hammer.

Find a piece of scrap wood that is in good condition. This wood can be stained, painted, or unfinished. If your wood is natural, you can stain it yourself, or paint it with diluted tempera paint to add a little bit of color and highlight the grain. The wood can stay rough or be sanded smooth.

Consider the size and shape of your piece of wood and start planning your design. Try to think in terms of rhythm. Have smooth lines that seem to flow into one another creating handsome, elegant shapes all in harmony. See if you can create a visual melody of smooth flowing spaces and lines. This preliminary design may be lightly sketched with crayon, chalk, or charcoal as a guideline for your finished design. As the lines overlap, they create shapes for your finished piece.

When you have planned the division of space to your satisfaction, it is time to interpret these flat areas into raised, gleaming metal shapes. Try to have available a wide selection of nails. You can use any type of nail of any size. Choose some with wide heads as well as slender finishing nails.

Fill in the drawn spaces you have created. Large areas may be filled with wide head nails, perhaps with some of them leading into another space filled with slender, sharp nails. Nails put together create a solid shape while those spaced wider apart can create a moving, flowing line. Plan carefully.

You can create different heights to your design according to how deeply you hammer in the nails. If only a couple of blows are used your nails will stand tall. If you like, you can contrast this with nails that are set deep. Your composition will take shape quickly and you'll begin to see how handsome your sculpture will be—as you create your design with a bang!

Make It Easy—for Yourself!

1. Have the class bring in natural wood (plain, stained, or painted) which is fairly soft. Avoid hard composition-type wood.
2. Start collecting nails long in advance to insure having enough for the class.
3. If not enough hammers are brought in, the nails can be pressed in by hand until a hammer is available to finish the design.
4. Keep the nails separated into their own groups and display them on a table. They may be placed in paper plates or cups.
5. Use a thick pad of newspaper under the wood to protect the desk and to help muffle the sound.

Variation

Lay a large Homasote panel on the floor. Paint it black or any dark color. Create a large non-objective mural by having each child make a freeform shape. Fill the spaces with different kinds of nails. Add areas of paper or fabric appliquéd with nails around the edges.

OBJECTIVES

1. To appreciate the value of scrap materials in creating an art object.

2. To learn to use line to create the illusion of space.

3. To develop a sense of rhythm in design.

(For Grades 3 through 6; adapted to Grades K through 2)

Lesson Two:

NAIL IT DOWN!

Non-objective Op Art

IS YOUR GARAGE OR ATTIC OR BASEMENT like most of them? If it is, you will be able to find some scraps of wood and some nails. Any size will do. You'll probably even find some string. Find a hammer, too. Then you can make a real op art design! How? Why, Just nail it down!

It may look as though we're getting ready to build a house—or more likely that we've just finished building one. But instead, we're going to take all these scraps and build a three-dimensional picture. It won't have anything real in it—just lines. We'll use the string for that.

How do you suppose we can make that string stand away from the wood—be three-dimensional, that is? Could the nails help us? Well, let's see. Hammer several nails into a piece of scrap wood just far enough so that they feel firm but so that part of each of them stands above the piece of wood.

Now you have something to attach the string to. Just tie one end to one of the nails. Like that. Now what can you do with it? Certainly—take the string to another nail, wrap it around the nail once or twice—and then on to another nail, and another, and another. Pull the string tight to make smooth, straight lines. See, you can make the lines go in any direction you want them to. Yes, you could even start at the bottom of the nail and make one layer over another. You can do all kinds of things, can't you?

Let each person have a piece of scrap wood and a handful of nails. Then close your ears while the hammering starts. Encourage the children to plan where they will place their nails. Remember, the nails are just to hold the string so it can make lines for the design. If you have colored string, plan the arrangement of colors. Don't stop too soon. Place the lines close together so that it looks almost like solid areas instead of just lines. Some of the lines even look rounded, don't they? It is like an optical illusion.

Finally the last nail will be in place and a wonderful quiet will return! Collect the hammers, put away the remaining nails and left-over string. Find a place to display each of the designs. You will find yourself fascinated by them—almost hypnotized by the rhythm of the lines.

Make It Easy—for Yourself!

1. Use irregular scraps of wood. The sizes may vary but approximately the size of your hand spread out is satisfactory.
2. Plan where the nails should be put. In order to create rhythmic, moving lines, at least most of the nails should be near the edges of the wood.
3. Colored string in some areas will add interest to the finished design. Yarn or embroidery cotton may be used in place of string. To create fine lines use sewing thread.
4. Several children may share a hammer if necessary.

Variations

1. Make a line design in a box. Any size box will do. Cut slits in the edges of the box, wherever you want a line to begin. If your design is made in a small box, use string or even thread. If your design is made in a large box, use yarn or cotton roving. Insert the string (or other line material) into the slits and carry from one slit to another.
2. Cut slits around the edges of a small piece of heavy cardboard. Make a line design by inserting thread or thin string into the slits and carrying from one to another. Use a brayer to roll tempera paint or waterbase block printing ink over the entire design. Place the inked plate over another paper and rub with your hand. Remove the plate and re-ink for as many prints as you want.

Variation for Lower Grades

Cut slits around the edges of a piece of heavy cardboard. Use colored yarn to create a line design. Insert the yarn into the slits and carry from one slit to another until there is a pleasing design.

O B J E C T I V E S

1. To use a solid material to create a three-dimensional construction.

2. To learn to see the possibilities for creative work in scrap materials.

3. To learn to create balance in a three-dimensional design.

(For Grades 4 through 6)

Lesson Three:

BUILDING BLOCKS

Wood Constructions

YOU KNOW HOW MUCH YOUNG CHILDREN like to play with building blocks. They make all kinds of things— from just towers that go up into the air to castles or trucks or anything their imaginations can invent. Well, older children will enjoy them, too, if they're not just plain ordinary blocks, but building blocks that come in all sizes and shapes.

Gather together a BIG collection of scrap wood. Be sure many of them are "chunks" of wood—thick pieces rather than just flat boards. Have as many shapes and sizes as possible—plain pieces, fancy pieces, big pieces, little pieces. Spread them out on the table (or even the floor) where they can be seen easily. Let the class stand in a group around them.

Now what are we going to do with those blocks? Well, blocks are to build with, to put together—so we'll put them together! Let's go modern this time and build some abstract structures. We won't let them look at all real, just an interesting construction made from interesting blocks.

Whenever you build anything you need a solid base—right? So select a rather large block to begin with. Choose one which is large enough to make a solid, stable base for the rest of the design. Let each child choose his beginning building block.

Take a good look at your block. Is there one place on your base or foundation that looks like a good place to start the design? Will it be right in the middle? Well, perhaps so, but probably not. Usually things look better—and a little less formal—if there is more variety than that. Can you find a second block that looks like just the right one to add to your base? Perhaps it will be a short, flat one that will look almost like a part of the base. Maybe it will be a rather tall one that will begin to add height right away to your design. But, whatever it is, choose a block which will make a good beginning for your construction. Make it one that you can add onto to give extra width and extra height.

169

Let everyone choose two or three more blocks that they like before they take them all back to their desks. Play around with the blocks for a while to see which way you want to arrange them. Get more blocks if you need to. Then glue them together to form a modern abstract structure.

As the children continue building their designs, walk about the room giving help. Does it begin to look too flat? Should you add height to it? Or do you want to make it a long, low structure? Be sure your design is sturdy, that it is strong and balanced. Perhaps you need another block near the base. See if you can find just the right one. You are making a three-dimensional construction, so be sure it looks good from all sides.

Continue building until each construction is finished. When each design looks just right, gather up the extra blocks. Save them for another day—you may want to build again.

Allow time for the glue to dry thoroughly. Then you may want to give your designs a couple of coats of varnish. They will be worth taking the extra time for that finishing touch. Have a special place of honor where you can take turns displaying each building block construction.

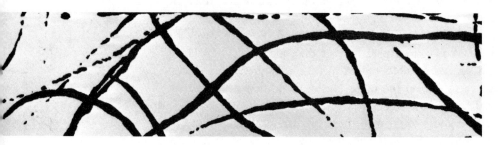

Make It Easy—for Yourself!

1. Have a large assortment of scrap wood. Be sure there is a large variety of sizes, from tiny pieces to pieces large and heavy enough to form the bases. Keep the constructions rather small so that glue will hold them together.
2. Cover the work areas with newspaper to protect the surface from the glue and the rough wood.
3. Use a quick drying glue to attach the parts of the construction. Hold the pieces to be glued firmly in place until the glue dries.

Variation

Make realistic objects from pieces of scrap wood.

OBJECTIVES

1. To give new life to an old technique.

2. To be more aware of the beauty of wood.

3. To teach wood grain-ing to children.

(For Grades K through 4)

Lesson Four:

TIME TO RESIST!

Crayon Resist on Wood

ARE YOU IN THE SAME OLD ART RUT? Are you using the same old lessons in the same old way? Are you falling into an uncreative conformity? Stop! It's time to resist!

171

It's time to resist—crayon resist, that is—in a new way. Out with the tired old underwater scenes. Out with the same old background papers— out dullness! Try resisting on wood! Yes, wood. Show your class that you don't have to always paint wood to finish it. Teach them about the beauty of staining wood. You can achieve all this in an easy lesson.

We must, of course, choose our piece of wood carefully. It can be an old plank or even a piece of plywood. In fact, small pieces of plywood are ideal for this lesson. Maybe you can get a lumber company to cut up some small squares of scrap, or perhaps you can have the class bring in pieces which can be cut and shared. Any unpainted or unstained wood may be used.

The lesson itself is rudimentary. First, see if the grain in the wood suggests a background for a picture. It may suggest clouds in a sky, wall-paper, outer space, or many other things. Draw a picture directly on the wood using bright colored wax crayons. Apply the crayon thickly, but leave quite a bit of the wood background showing.

Take some diluted tempera paint—or commercial fabric dye, or colored inks—and brush over the entire wood surface, going in the direction of the grain. The picture will remain undisturbed while the background will absorb the color like a stain. Because the grain will absorb the color it will not be covered as in painted wood. Instead, all the beauty and highlights of the grain will be enhanced.

Imagine the delight of the children as they see the background of their pictures take on a new beauty and life. You'll be so glad it was time to resist!

Make It Easy—for Yourself!

1. Emphasize the beauty of the wood so that the crayon picture will not be too dominant.
2. Cover the desks with paper—especially when using dye.
3. Brush on paint or dye in the same direction as the grain. Start at the top of the picture and overlap each band of color.
4. Test the thickness of the paint. Remember it should soak into the wood, not cover it.

Variation

Follow the natural lines of the grain to fill the in between spaces with crayon. Cover with dye or thin paint for an interesting non-objective design. This is especially effective on large pieces of wood.

OBJECTIVES

1. To open a new dimension in painting.

2. To present a craft-like lesson that has a personal touch.

3. To highlight the use of mixed media in art.

4. To appreciate the art possibilities of discarded materials.

(For Grades 5 and 6)

Lesson Five:

OPEN A GIFT SHOP

Wall Plaques

ART IS FAST BECOMING A PERSONAL THING TO millions of people. It is no longer relegated to just the museum, but it is entering the homes in unusual, decorative, and entertaining ways. You and your class can create wall plaques, for example, so beautiful that you will want to open a gift shop!

It is often not so much the nature of the painting which is striking but the combinations of materials used in the artistic work. Here is a practical suggestion which can lead to a most rewarding experience for children. It will, as well, let them create a most unique and handsome gift.

If we search the cellar, garage, or attic, we're bound to discover a piece of an old discarded board. As long as it is not painted we can use it for our painting. We must clean it to get rid of any dirt or blemishes. This can be done simply with soap and water. When it is dry we paint a picture on it. We may use thick tempera paint or ordinary house paints. Our picture must fit the size of our board for we don't want it either too overbearing or too tiny. The drawing may be done in charcoal, chalk, or even crayon. Keep it simple and devoid of too many details, for we want a pleasant, almost primitive, decorative effect.

Paint the picture in flat colors, but don't use too many of them. Three or four will be plenty for our purposes. Leave much of the background showing. Consider still lifes of fruit, vegetable, flowers, or dried grasses as your subject, or you may prefer something like a bird, fish, butterfly, a sailing ship, or an ancient artifact.

Make one simple object rather than a picture crammed with small and insignificant parts.

When the painting is absolutely dry, varnish only the painted surface. Allow it to dry thoroughly. Then choose a dark stain and go over the entire board. The unpainted surface will take on a beautiful glow as the grain shows through, and the painted part of the picture will look antiqued. Two coats of stain may be applied for a deeper color. If the stain is too dark and disturbs the colors too much, you may want to wipe it off the painted and varnished surface.

Try to find an interesting piece of wood—one that perhaps has turned gray with age or exposure, or one that has been broken so that it has a sharp, jagged end. These pictures may be made vertical or horizontal.

All you need now are some price tags and you will be able to open a gift shop!

Make It Easy—for Yourself!

1. Don't try to complete this lesson in one period. Drawing and painting should be done during the same art lesson. The varnishing may be done in small groups or on an individual basis, followed by another period for staining.

2. Cover desks thoroughly when using stains and varnish.
3. Don't use wood which has been varnished. The stain will not penetrate to color the wood.
4. Use large pieces of wood for more dramatic paintings.
5. Don't use watercolor brushes for staining or varnishing. They can be cleaned but they will lose their soft supple quality.
6. Be sure to stain the edges of the board. This can be done with two or three coats for a darker border.
7. A notch in the center of the back can be dug out for a way of hanging the picture—or picture loops and wire may be used.
8. If you want a shiny finish, revarnish after staining.
9. Use turpentine to clean brushes that have been in stain and varnish.

Variations

1. Use long, wide boards the same length, nailed together with small cross pieces, to make a large wooden mural. Large sheets of plywood can also be used for a mural.
2. Tissue paper, construction paper, or fabric can be glued over stained wood to make a picture. Varnish (two coats) over the completed picture for a handsome finish.

OBJECTIVES

1. To create a three-dimensional, architectural structure.

2. To help develop a sense of rhythm and balance through use of line and space.

3. To create a feeling of added depth by overlapping spaces.

4. To realize that discarded materials can be used to create interesting art objects.

(For Grades 4 through 6; adapted to Grades 2 and 3)

Lesson Six:

BOXED IN

Building with Boxes

HAVE YOU EVER BEEN BOXED IN? OH,
you've felt that way lots of times! But have you ever—really and truly—
been boxed in? Well, let's try it.

Prepare for the lesson by having the children bring in boxes of every
size. You will need big boxes (about the size 12″ x 18″ drawing paper
comes in is good), middle size boxes, little boxes, tiny boxes. Have the
children look through their garages, attics, basements—or any other part
of the house. Even a nearby candy store may save the boxes popular candy
bars come in—they make a wonderful assortment of sizes and shapes.
You'll need fat boxes and skinny boxes, tall boxes and short boxes—the
more boxes the better!

Begin the lesson by talking about modern architecture. Are there some
new buildings in your neighborhood or a nearby city? What do they look
like? Well, probably they're made mostly of straight lines—of rectangles.
Perhaps the whole building is one large rectangle with smaller ones inside
it. Most modern architecture is like that. Look around your own classroom.
It is almost certainly a series of straight-line shapes.

What things can you find right in this room that are made of straight
lines—that are rectangles? Of course, the blackboards are. That's right!
The windows, the bulletin boards, the teacher's desk, the children's desks.
And many other things, too. Probably the fluorescent lights are encased in
cube-like structures. The cupboards, the bookcases, the doors all make rectangular shapes.

Most modern architecture is made up of a series of box-like structures.
So let's go modern—and make an architectural structure.

Take a large box (the top has been cut off so that one side is open)
and several smaller boxes—perhaps the cover of a shoe box and the box
some candy bars have come in. Let's start by standing our large box on
end so our building will be as tall as possible—or, of course, you could have
a long, low building. Now, let's see—what can we do with these two boxes
to break up that big, plain space inside the big box? Well, we can put them
anywhere at all—just attach them inside to some part of the big box. But

if one just goes in front of the other, like that, would that look good? Not at all! So let's move them around until they look just right. Perhaps the open side of the candy box could face us and be attached to this side of the box. Then the closed top of the shoe box might overlap in front of it and be attached to the top of the big box. There, now we have several new shapes already.

Move the boxes around until they make pleasing new shapes. Try to create a feeling of depth by overlapping rectangles and by having some open and some closed sides of boxes facing you. Place the first boxes near—but not touching—the back of the large box that forms the outside framework of your structure. This will leave the middle and front part of the opening for further development of your structure—your three-dimensional design.

When your first boxes have been arranged, glue them in place. Oh, of course it will be necessary to hold them until the glue dries, won't it? Otherwise the structure would fall apart!

By now each child will be eager to begin his own architectural structure. Give each child a large box for his framework, and let him choose two or three boxes to begin his design. Have the boxes arranged on a counter top or table so that the children may choose more boxes whenever they need them. Each child should have his own tube of glue.

Walk about the room as the structures begin to develop. Be sure you begin near the back of your large box. Keep the new shapes near the back. Then you can add more boxes in front of the others.

Encourage the children to step back away from their work and see it from a distance. That way you can really see where there is an empty area that needs another box. Have you tried putting a smaller box inside a larger one? There are all sizes of boxes, you know. Oh, no, no, don't take tiny boxes yet! Those are the last ones to use. They would just be covered up if you used them first.

Try to get as much depth to your structure as possible. Some open and some closed areas overlapping each other will help make your design look even more three-dimensional.

That's the way to do it! Arrange the boxes so that they create interesting new shapes. Perhaps just a tiny box inside one of these shapes in the front would finish your whole design. See if you can find just the right box.

Finally all the architectural structures will be finished. You will really be boxed in—but in what a delightful way! Let groups of children take turns walking about the room to examine and admire each structure.

Display them, of course! How? Why, that's easy! Each structure may be displayed separately—on top of a bookcase, in an empty corner of the room, on the back of the library table, in the hall display case, on a counter top—in any space at all. Or display them all together as a three-dimensional mural. Place each structure tight against the next one—even a double layer of them. You will be surprised. Each structure will become part of a whole new architectural structure.

Make It Easy—for Yourself!

1. Have one large box for each person. This forms the frame of the architectural structure. Boxes about the size 12″ x 18″ drawing paper comes in are fine. A nearby grocery store may be able to furnish you with a similar size.
2. Have a wide variety of sizes and shapes of boxes. Have them from shoe box size to tiny ones that are lipstick size.
3. Let each child choose three or four boxes to begin his structure. This will get everyone working quickly. Then allow the children to choose boxes of the right size and shape as they are needed.
4. Encourage the children to use the large and middle size boxes first. Save the tiny ones for the last. They add the accents, the notes of interest. If they are used earlier in the lesson, they will be lost as larger boxes are placed in front of them.
5. Use a strong, quick drying glue or cement. Even with these it will be necessary to hold each box firmly in place until the glue hardens. Glue may damage the surface of desks, so stress the importance of keeping glue inside the structure when it is not in use.

6. Encourage children frequently to stand away from their structures and view them from a distance. By doing this they will be able to see where—or if—other boxes are needed. (It will be easier for the children to work if they stand all during the lesson.)

7. The learning part of the lesson is the choice and arrangement of the boxes—the making of the structure. Painting the finished product is an extra—to be done only if you want to. The advertising on the boxes will not detract from the finished product. If you do want to paint the structure, do it in dull colored tempera paint with few if any bright colors in order to keep the structural effect that has been created.

8. There will be no real cleanup. Put away the tubes of glue and throw out the extra boxes (or save them for another lesson).

Variation

Create a completely in-the-round structure. Use a wide, low box for the base and build upward from it rather than in it. Turn the structure continually so that it is pleasing when viewed from any direction.

Variation for Lower Grades

Use boxes to create imaginary people and animals. Paint them (with tempera paint) to make them funny, fierce, angry—or whatever mood you like. Add bits of felt, cloth, string, yarn, paper, buttons for details.

OBJECTIVES

1. To combine two- and three-dimensional art in a single activity.

2. To provide opportunity to select from a wide variety of scrap material in order to create an original art project.

3. To encourage children to adapt materials to new uses.

4. To provide opportunity for combining art with other subject areas.

(For Grades 3 through 6)

Lesson Seven:

LET'S GO TO THE THEATER

Dioramas

HOW WOULD YOU LIKE TO SEE A STORY INSTEAD OF hearing it? How would you like to see your social studies lesson instead of reading it? Well, let's go to the theater—our own, that is—and then we *can* see all these things.

181

We'll make our theater—lots of them in fact. They can be theaters that are starring our favorite characters, they can be showing the latest—and original—dramas, or there can be "re-runs" of a story we've read before. Our dioramas—or theaters—can show anything we want them to.

Before you begin the lesson, be sure you have collected all the materials you will need. The most important thing you will need is a box for each diorama that is to be made. This will form the stage. Then, of course, you will need all the things for making the scenery and the characters. You can use almost anything for that: all kinds of paper, cloth of various colors and textures (both plain and print), non-hardening clay, twigs, sticks, cardboard tubes, shells, yarn, roving, string, wire, felt, leather, old jewelry, knicknacks and junk of all varieties. Bring in anything you can get; you will find a use for it!

There are only a few things you will need to discuss with your class before they begin their own dioramas. First of all—what are you going to be "showing" at your theater? Perhaps you would like to have each child choose his own subject, and then you will have a wide variety of productions. Or perhaps you would rather have them all related. In that case, decide upon a subject: fairy tales, book reports, a social studies correlation, original stories.

Now—everybody have an idea? Fine! Let's begin our production. Plan just what you want to be in your scene. Will there be people, animals, buildings, trucks? Will it be an indoor or outdoor scene? Will it be in the city, country, at the seashore? It can be any place you want it to be that is appropriate to your subject. You have to know just where it is, though, so that you can plan your background.

Let's think about that background for a minute. The rectangular sides of that box don't look good, do they? Besides, no place, except perhaps the inside of a room, would have just straight sides like that. So our first job is to get rid of those uninteresting edges. Can you think of any way of doing that? A rounding line (somebody may even have a round hat box) would look better, wouldn't it? Yes, you could attach a piece of paper to the front edge of the box, carry it back, rounding off the corner, continue it across the back, round off the other corner, carrying it to the front where you attach it opposite the original starting point. See, no corners any more!

Talk for a few minutes about some of the materials that have been collected. Children will have wonderful ideas about what they can be used for: sponges for tree tops and bushes, real twigs to use for tree trunks or winter trees, clothespins or pipe cleaners for bodies of people, to be finished with cloth or paper, cotton batting for snow or clouds, non-hardening clay to model almost anything.

Don't expect your dioramas to be finished in a hurry. It takes time to plan, to design the background, to make each item, and to assemble it all in a stage setting. But whatever time it takes will be well worth it when you decide to go to the theater—a whole room full of them.

Make It Easy—for Yourself!

1. Children may work individually or in small groups.
2. Display available materials where they can be easily seen so as to encourage creative use of them. Allow the children to return as often as necessary to obtain materials.
3. Have glue available to use with non-porous materials. Paste is satisfactory to use on paper or fabric.
4. No pencils—they discourage free, creative work.
5. Avoid ready-made articles. Children's creative use of materials will be more satisfying.

Variation

Fold a piece of 12" x 18" construction paper or oak tag into three equal parts (12" x 6"). Tape the ends together so as to form a triangular form. Cut a large oval from one side. This will provide an opening into the shape and become the basis for a simple diorama.

OBJECTIVES

1. To use a "found" material, as part of an art lesson.

2. To capitalize on the imaginations of young children.

3. To encourage children to be creative with simple materials.

(For Grades K through 3)

Lesson Eight:

"ONCE UPON A TIME"

Imaginary Pictures

DO THE WORDS, "ONCE UPON A TIME..." start your mind working? Do you see far-away places, strange creatures, and unusual sights? Let's go on an imaginary trip that starts with "Once upon a time"!

You won't need any magic carpet for this trip—only a large cardboard carton. Perhaps a furniture or appliance store will give you one that a refrigerator or stove came in. That would be just great, but if you're not lucky enough to get one like that, any large box will do. Set it in a corner of your classroom so that the open part of the box faces the wall. Leave just enough space for a child to walk through and into the box.

You're not really walking into a box—you're going into a place of "once upon a time." Perhaps it will be a castle. Maybe you will see kings and queens and knightly lords! Perhaps you will even be changed into one of them. Wouldn't that be fun!

Ask who is brave enough to venture into this strange land of make-believe. You'll have lots of volunteers. Your adventurer may want to close his eyes when he gets inside so that he can really "see" better. Perhaps he is in a cave with all kinds of strange creatures around him. It must be a scary place!

But the next person will find a different place of "once upon a time." Let several children take turns walking into the mystery box. Urge each child to explore a different place: a cave, a forest, a castle, a mine, a pirate ship, a cavern, a land below the sea. Let each one tell about what he saw. You will be amazed by youthful imaginations.

After three or four explorers have returned from their adventures, let them have a large paper and a box of crayons so that they may show what they saw on their journeys. One at a time each child will have his turn to enter the land of "once upon a time." After everyone has had a chance to explore, let anyone who wants to make a return trip to his own special place.

You may want to have each child write a short description of his visit to go along with his picture. There will be no end to the variety of "once upon a time."

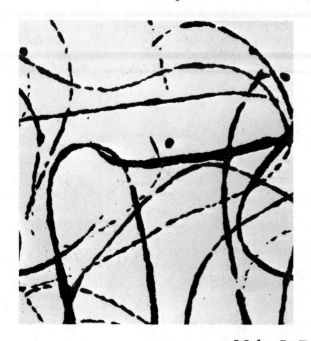

Make It Easy—for Yourself!

1. Have as large a box as possible. It will be best if a child can stand upright in it—even move about slightly. If a box is not available, drape a sheet over a table.
2. Use large paper—at least 12 x 18.
3. No pencils! They encourage small, tight work.
4. The youngest children will have to dictate their stories while you write them.

Variation

Have several medium size boxes in which you have placed an object or picture which will start imaginations. Let each child decide which box to look into—then make a picture of his land of make-believe.

OBJECTIVES

1. To introduce weaving as an art form.

2. To use line as the important element in creating an interesting design.

3. To help to develop manual dexterity.

4. To use color to create unity in a design.

(For Grades 4 through 6; adapted to Grades 2 and 3)

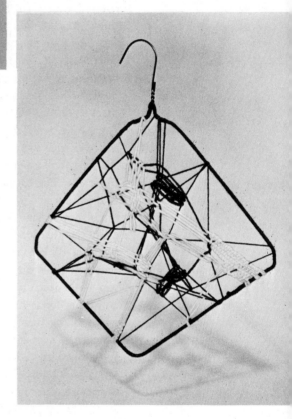

Lesson Nine:

LET'S BE SPIDERS!

Woven Mobiles

DID YOU EVER LOOK CLOSELY AT A SPIDER WEB? Perhaps you admired the delicately woven lines, the intricate patterns. Then you brushed it all away—for who wants a spider web around? Well,

187

we do—the kind, that is, that we're going to make. So let's be spiders!

You'll need only a few things for each person: a wire coathanger, a ball of yarn, a bobby pin, a pair of scissors.

A real spider would have to make the outside edge of his web, but we're not that clever. So we'll just take a wire coathanger and pull the long horizontal piece down from the middle until the hanger is almost diamond shaped with the hook at the top. Now take a long piece of yarn. How long? Oh, more than a yard long. Tie one end of it to the coathanger and begin to wrap it tightly around the wire. Around and around and around—wrap it around until all of the diamond shaped wire has been covered with yarn. Sure it will take a while but not really as long as you think. And besides, spiders are patient—and so are we!

Have another coathanger that you have previously wound with yarn. That way you can show the class how to begin to wind the wire—and then, presto, it is all finished! How do you suppose you could begin to spin the inside of a spider web? Certainly—you need lines across your shape. Well, that's easy. Just tie another piece of the same color yarn to your frame (or use the end of what was left over from winding it) and carry it across the open area to another part of the frame. Wind it once completely around the wire, and then carry it back across the open area to another part of the frame. There, that was easy, wasn't it? But is that enough, do you think? No, no, not at all! So just continue to make lines across the design. Sometimes a new line will go on top of another one, sometimes it will go under another one. Make the lines go in all directions until the whole space is broken into interesting shapes—some large, some small. Each time you make a new line be sure to wind the yarn completely around the wire—not just around the outside edge, but one complete turn around it.

That looks pretty good, doesn't it? But no spider would ever leave a web looking that way—and we're not going to, either! Perhaps you have done some weaving before this. If you have, you know that when you weave you make a thread go over, under, over, under other threads. We'll weave a spider web by making another piece of yarn go over, under, over, under the threads that are already here.

Tie another piece of yarn—the same color or a different one—to the frame. Insert it through the parts of a bobby pin as though you were threading a needle. Decide which area you want to weave, and carry the thread across open areas, weaving over and under any threads that are already there. There, now, that's enough of that! It is time for all of you to become spiders.

There will be plenty for you to do while the webs are being woven. There's someone who has forgotten to pull the wire into a diamond first. Someone else is in too much of a hurry and is winding the wire too loosely. That wouldn't look good, would it? Just twist it until it is tight—then pull the end of the yarn. See, it takes less yarn, too, when you do a good job. Oops, don't change colors until you have a framework inside the diamond. The same color yarn inside as outside helps to bring your eye into the design—not just keep it on the outside.

That makes a good color combination—just two varieties of the same color. That's a good one, too, with a dark color and a light color. Oh, don't stop yet! Fill some more areas. Be a patient spider, weaving back and forth until some parts are filled rather solidly and other parts are still open and lace-like. Tie another long thread whenever it is needed.

Finally even the slowest spider will be finished! These webs are not to be brushed away, so how can you display them? Well, how about making one giant web by putting them all together? Hook one of them over a nail, from a light fixture, from any projection at all. Then use the hook on each design to attach it to another design until a giant spider web is created. Let it be a free-hanging mobile or arrange it on a large bulletin board with colored paper in the background. No real spider ever wove a web as big and as beautiful as that!

Make It Easy—for Yourself!

1. If possible, see that each child has his own ball of yarn to begin with and that there are a few extras. When the diamond shape has been covered all with one color and the beginning lines have been formed, children may leave their balls of yarn at a sharing area and take another color. Balls of yarn may be shared, however, if that much yarn cannot be obtained. In that way there will always be a good variety of colors available.

2. Pull the yarn fairly taut both while winding the wire and while forming the beginning lines on which the weaving will be done.

3. Wrap the yarn *completely* around the wire each time. This will hold it in place and keep it from slipping.

4. The whole design may be completed with a single color, but be certain that the color with which the wire frame is covered is also used to begin the lines for weaving. This will carry the outside color into the center of the design and help create a unified whole.

5. When attaching another piece of yarn, tie a secure knot. Try to cover the end pieces of yarn with some part of the design.

Variations

1. Use doorbell wire to create a three-dimensional freeform shape. Doorbell wire is coated and so will not need to be covered with yarn. Finish the design in the same way as was done with the coathanger frame. In this case there will be several areas in which you create designs, and so the whole will be a three-dimensional "spider web."

2. Make a "spider web" mural on a bulletin board. Place thumbtacks at intervals of two or three inches around the edges of the bulletin board. Let children take turns creating the design. First make lines across the whole area, from around one thumb tack to and around another. Make sure they create an interesting line design. Then use the lines to weave over and under, filling some areas fairly solid and leaving others open. When the mural is finished, remove the thumb tacks that were not used. You may want to use a heavier yarn for this giant "spider web," perhaps cotton roving or any bulky yarn.

3. Make a spatial design inside a box. Push holes through each side of a box from which the cover has been removed. Put some of the holes close together—in straight or curved lines. Carry a thread back and forth from holes on one side to holes on another side. Create "areas" by carrying the thread back and forth on lines of holes and by crossing over them with lines in the opposite directions. Use the holes near the back of the box first, or else they will be out of reach as the front part of the design is completed. Use any size box. In tiny boxes create the spatial design with colored sewing thread; for larger boxes use colored string or yarn; for giant boxes use cotton roving or bulky yarn.

Variations for Lower Grades

1. Weave with paper strips. Cut 9" x 12" colored construction paper into 12" strips of various widths—quarter-inch, half-inch, inch. Make a paper loom by folding in half a piece of 12" x 18" white or colored construction paper. Cut it into inch-wide slits beginning on the folded edge and extending to within an inch of the opposite open edges. Unfold the cut paper and you will have a loom on which to weave the strips. Plan colors and various widths in an over, under, over, under woven pattern that creates an interesting woven design.
2. Cut cardboard into any easy-to-handle sizes. Make notches or slits around the four sides. Insert yarn into one of the notches, carry it to a notch on another side—then another and another. Continue until the design is completed.

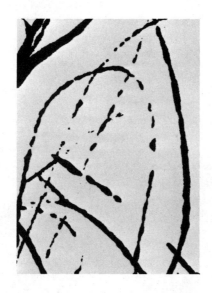

OBJECTIVES

1. To use an accidental form of art to stimulate imaginations.

2. To learn to visualize parts of a picture which are not already on paper.

3. To have a fun experience in art.

(For Grades 1 through 4)

Lesson Ten:

LET THE STRING TELL YOU

String Pictures

IT'S ALWAYS FUN TO MAKE A PICTURE, BUT especially so when you can let the string tell you what to make. It's a lazy way to make a picture—but lots of fun, too.

How can you let a piece of string tell you what to make? Drop the string—or yarn—on a piece of 12" x 18" drawing paper. Does that make you think of anything? Is there the beginning of a picture there? Perhaps someone will see two eyes. That could be the beginning of a face, couldn't it? Turn the paper in a different direction. It will look different that way. Yes, it could be a clown's shoe. Then you would have to draw the rest of the clown, wouldn't you? We'll use crayons for that. Of course, we'd have to paste down the string first so it would stay in just the right place.

Drop the string two or three times more. Each time try to find several things that the string reminds you of. Talk about the other things that would have to be added to finish the picture. Let two or three children try it.

But enough of that! Let's make our own pictures, and let the string tell us what it is going to be. Give each person a large piece of paper and a string. Now, drop it—and see what the string tells you. Yes, there's one that is the helmet of a spaceman. You can do all kinds of things with that. Where is the spaceman? What is he doing? Then put a little paste under the string so that it will stay right there. Then you can use your crayons to finish the rest of the picture.

As you walk about the room let the children tell you what they have found. Encourage them to talk about what the string is and what they are going to add. There will be all kinds of things from spacemen to butterflies and from trucks to turtles. Encourage the children to give their pictures titles.

Display each picture, for each will have its own special charm. How else could you have gotten such wonderful pictures except by letting the string tell you!

Make It Easy—for Yourself!

1. Use a piece of string about fifteen inches long. Hold it at least a foot or two above the paper before dropping it. Let the shape in which it falls be entirely accidental.
2. While the children are dropping their pieces of string, give each person a small amount of paste and a paste brush. If paste brushes are not available, each child may make an applicator by folding a piece of scrap paper several times, then folding it in the middle.
3. As you walk around the room during the lesson, collect the extra paste and the brushes as soon as individual children have finished with them. This provides more working space and makes for an easier clean-up at the end of the lesson.
4. Encourage children to press hard with their crayons so as to make brighter colors and more interesting pictures.
5. If you use light-colored string, have the children outline it with a bright or dark crayon so that the line it creates will stand out in the picture.

Variation

Use colored paper instead of string and crayons. Tear an accidental shape from a piece of colored paper. Drop it on a piece of drawing paper. "Find" the beginning of a picture in it. Tear other shapes to complete the picture. Paste to the drawing paper.

OBJECTIVES

1. To use paint in a new way.

2. To use line as an important element of design.

3. To realize that even a partly "accidental" picture must be planned.

(For Grades 4 through 6; adapted to Grades 1 through 3)

Lesson Eleven:

DROP IT!

Painting with String

YOU HAVE CERTAINLY PAINTED WITH brushes. Probably you have painted with your hands—and perhaps even with sponges. But have you ever painted with string? You won't even have to brush it. All you need to do is—drop it!

195

Have your class stand around you as you demonstrate. Cover a table with newspaper, and have a small quantity of thin tempera paint in paper cups. Include a dark color (perhaps black), a light color (perhaps white), and three or four bright colors (perhaps red, blue, green, and yellow). Several colors of 12″ x 18″ construction paper will be needed, too. In addition, have a piece of string about 18 or 20 inches long for each color of paint. Show the class the materials and the colors that are available to them.

Now let's see what we can do with these things. Certainly if I'm going to paint with string, I'll have to get the paint on it. So I'll just dip a piece of string into each color of paint. But I will want to hold on to the string and not get the paint all over my fingers. So I'll just hold on to each end of the string like this. Fold the string in half with both ends even so that you can hold them together. Now place the middle end of the string into one of the paper cups of paint. Use a tongue depressor to put the string into the paint. But I'll leave the ends out and hanging over the edge of the cup so that they will stay clean. See, like that. Do the same thing with each of the other colors, putting a piece of string in each one—always leaving the ends of the string hanging over the edge of the cup so that they will stay clean.

I'll choose a piece of construction paper for my painting. Now I'll choose a color of paint that will show up well on it. Hold both ends of the string in one hand and use the tongue depressor to push the rest of the string into the paint. There, now I'm all ready to paint. Lift out the string, one end in each hand. Looks like it is going to drip, doesn't it? I don't want any paint to drop on my picture, so I'll just touch the middle of the string—where that drop is—to the newspaper. It won't do any harm there, will it? Now the string comes over my paper and I carefully drop it— the center first, then the two ends. I can put the string any place I want to. I can make it drop in a straight line—or I can curve the ends so that it drops in a rounding line. Oh, I don't need to drop the ends of the string. There's no paint on them, so I'll just hold on to them, and then I'll carefully pick up the rest of the string again.

And see what happened! There is the line that my string painted. Well, let's try it again. But this time I won't dip it into the paint— there's plenty still on the string. Do you think I should drop the string in the same place again? Of course not! That would be silly, wouldn't it? Shall I make the same kind of line as the last time? No, that would be silly, too. So I'll make a different shape this time. As I lay the string down I'll let it make a different kind of line. It even might have a circle in it, like that. I must be careful, too, about lifting up the string so it won't move and make a line where I don't want it to be.

Continue doing this over and over again, each time making a different kind of line on a different part of the paper. The line, of course, will get thinner and thinner as more paint is removed from the string. But that doesn't do any harm, does it? Just makes it more interesting by having variety. See, in some places the string didn't print at all.

It's time to go now to a second color of paint. But first put this string back into the paper cup it came from. Hold on to both ends, and let them hang over the side of the cup. There, now let's choose a second color, one that looks good with the paper and the paint I have already used.

Repeat the painting for a second and a third color. Fill the whole paper with lines. Let some of them extend right off your picture and onto the newspaper. Have a variety of kinds of lines, and balance the colors over the paper. Try to repeat some of the lines.

Perhaps you can think of an interesting title for the picture. Does it remind you of something? Can you see the beginning of a real thing in it? Or does it create a mood? *Sparklers in the Night*—yes, that would be fine! When you make your picture, try to think of a title that just belongs to your picture.

Arrange the class as you would for a regular painting lesson so that a group of children can share the same materials. Pass out the paper by colors, letting each child choose the one he wants. As soon as a child has his background paper he may begin painting.

String painting is easy and the results are partly accidental—that is one of the things that makes it fun. But the real success of it is in the planning—of colors, of shapes of lines and where they are placed. So encourage children to choose color which will contrast with their papers. Remind them to touch the drop of paint at the end of the string to their newspaper so that it won't drip on their pictures. Just that one drop, though. Don't waste the rest of the paint on the newspaper. And, oh, drop that string slowly so that you can plan the kind of shape it will make.

Let the pictures dry while the children clean up the work areas. Then have a quick showing. Good titles will make good pictures even better—and much more meaningful.

Make It Easy—for Yourself!

1. Have a limited number of colors of construction paper and paint —enough to give each child plenty of choice, but not so many that they become difficult to handle.
2. Arrange your room as you would for a painting lesson. A good plan is to group four or six desks together into one work area.

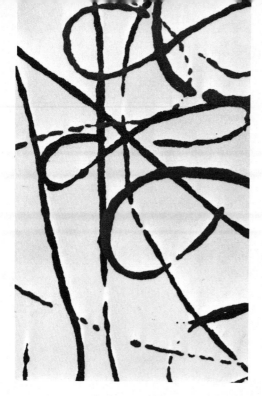

Have one desk for supplies only, shared by three or five children. If there is not enough desk, table, or counter space, one group could work on the floor.

3. Cover all work areas with newspaper.
4. Paper cups make good containers for the paint as they can be thrown away without any washing. They are light, however, and tip easily. Therefore, put only a small amount of paint in them in case they tip.
5. Picking up the string is as important as laying it down. If the string moves as it is picked up (or after it first touches the paper), it will make an unpleasant smudge. So pick the string up with the same line motions as it was put down with.
6. Hold on to the ends of the string all the time you are working with it.
7. Have the children stand to do their painting.
8. Clean up the easy way. Have a helper from each group bring the paper cups of paint to you—one color at a time as you direct. Lay the strings on a piece of newspaper, pour the excess paint back into the jars, and stack the empty paper cups. When all the paint has been collected, wrap the strings and paper cups in a piece of newspaper and discard them. Have each child slip his piece of newspaper out from under his picture and fold the newspaper a couple of times. Then the helper from each group may put them in the basket.

Variations

1. After the string painting has been finished, let each child choose one color of chalk—a color that he used in his painting. Make quick strokes with the chalk that repeat part of a painted line, then let the chalk stroke make an abrupt change in direction. This adds similar lines while also adding variety.
2. Use a tube of glue to draw a glue line similar to the dropped string lines. While the glue is still wet, lay a line of yarn or cotton roving into the glue. Repeat several times with the same color and then with other colors just as was done with the paint.

Variation for Lower Grades

Make only one dropped string line. Turn the paper in all directions until the beginning of an object is "found." Then complete the picture with crayons. One paint area could be arranged and the children could take turns using it.

from the

BACK

YARD

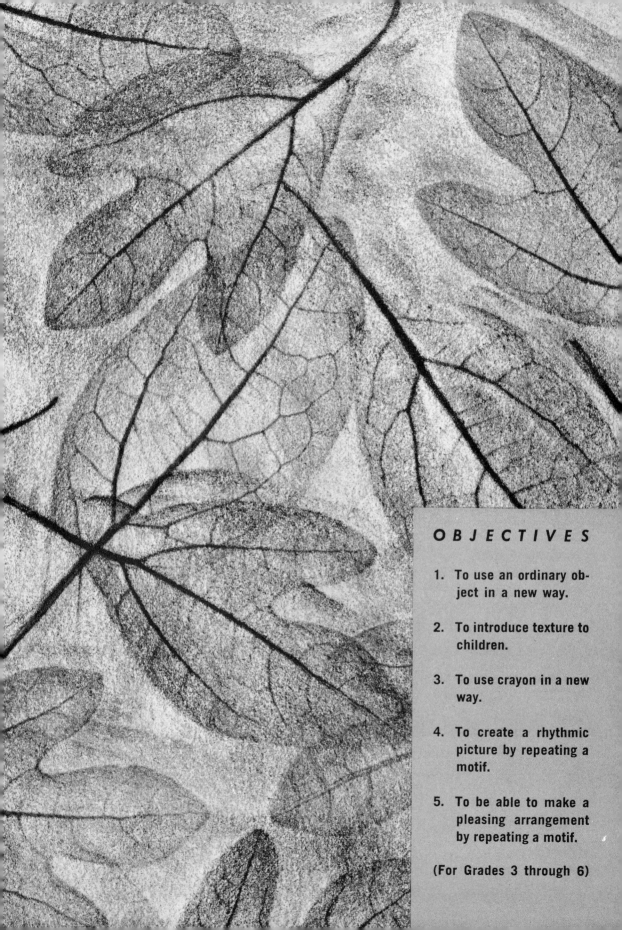

OBJECTIVES

1. To use an ordinary object in a new way.

2. To introduce texture to children.

3. To use crayon in a new way.

4. To create a rhythmic picture by repeating a motif.

5. To be able to make a pleasing arrangement by repeating a motif.

(For Grades 3 through 6)

Lesson One:

LEAVES, LEAVES EVERYWHERE!

Rubbed Crayon Textures

IN AUTUMN THE LEAVES FALL IN great cloudbursts. They cover the ground—you rake them, you burn them, you cart them away. They're a nuisance—there seem to be leaves, leaves everywhere!

Well, let's make use of a few of them. One or two leaves for each child will be enough. Other materials you will need are newspapers, 12" x 18" white or manila drawing paper, wax crayons.

Have your class gather about you while you demonstrate. Notice first that the leaves look—and feel—different on the two sides. One side is smooth, isn't it? And the other side is rough! Hide the leaf, rough side up, under a piece of 12" x 18" drawing paper. Even though you can't see the leaf, you can tell where it is because you can feel it. Rub your fingers across it.

Now take a wax crayon that has had the paper peeled from it. Lay it FLAT on the paper over the leaf. Press firmly on it and rub it across the paper. And look! There is the leaf—at least a print of it—right on top of the paper! See the outline of the edge of the leaf, and all the tiny veins through it.

Well, let's try it again. Move the leaf slightly. It can be a little separated from the print or it can overlap it. Rub the crayon across it again. Oh, the crayon has to be absolutely flat against the paper. Rub way out beyond the edges of the leaf. Don't worry about the extra crayon smudges. They will become a part of the picture. There's that same leaf a second time!

Continue to move and to rub the leaf several more times. Or perhaps you would like to have two leaves in your design. One might be larger than the other. Or what else could you do to add variety? Of course. You could use two different kinds of leaves. One might have a fancy edge— like a pin oak—and the other one might have a rather plain outline— like an elm leaf. Right! You might even use two different colors of crayons.

But would it be a good idea to use several different kinds of leaves and also several different colors? No! No! That would be a mess, wouldn't it? There would be so many different things that it wouldn't look good. So when you make your picture just use one or two or maybe three colors and one or two different leaves.

After you have an interesting arrangement of rubbed leaves all over your picture, you will want to fill in the extra places where crayon marks show beyond each leaf. That isn't any problem at all! Just take a different color of crayon, lay it on the side—just as you have done before—and rub over all the places between the leaves. Rub every place where there isn't already a color. Even overlap some of the other colors to make a more pleasing change from one color to another.

When the children have returned to their own desks, pass out newspaper to cover work areas so that crayon won't get on desk tops. Each person will also need a piece of 12″ x 18″ drawing paper as well as one or more leaves and crayons. Let them make their own choices.

Keep those crayons flat—don't draw with the ends of them. That's the way! Be sure the crayon rubs beyond the edge of the leaf so that the whole leaf shows. Compliment a child on his good choice of colors—or his pleasing arrangement—or his rubbed crayon technique. Urge the children to fill—but not crowd—the paper, letting some of the shapes go off the edges of the paper.

There they are—all finished. You'll have more leaves than ever, but they will be lovely ones that you will want to display—not burn or cart away like ordinary leaves.

Make It Easy—for Yourself!

1. Use leaves that you pick fresh from the tree—not those that have fallen to the ground for they are apt to be dry and brittle. Place the fresh leaves between the pages of a magazine. That will keep them flat and easier to use.
2. Use leaves that are of medium size. Leaves that are unusually

large or unusually small will be more difficult to work into a pleasing arrangement.

3. Have a variety of kinds of leaves to choose from.

4. Old, odd bits of crayons work as well as newer, better ones. Remove the paper from them. Or if newer crayons are used, remove the paper only half way down the crayon. This will give enough uncovered area (an inch or more) to lay flat on the paper.

5. There will be little clean-up. Have one child collect the crayons while another collects the leaves. Have each child slide out his newspaper and fold it in half. Then they can be collected and thrown away.

Variations

1. Use other "found" materials to make texture prints: yarn, string, pieces of corrugated paper.

2. Make texture rubbings of objects in the classroom. Lay a paper over the texture and take several rubbings of the same texture— perhaps with several colors. Add rubbings of other textures to the same picture.

3. Cut from another paper (heavier, if possible) other shapes. They may be realistic or non-objective. Use them in the same way as the leaves were used.

4. Make a realistic scene by cutting all the parts from heavy paper. Arrange them under a paper and rub them with the side of the crayon. Parts may be repeated if they are needed more than once in the picture.

5. Cut a 9" x 12" paper into rectangular pieces—some long and narrow, some almost square. Arrange them in an angular design. Cover with another paper and rub with crayon.

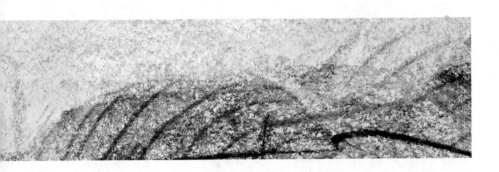

OBJECTIVES

1. To introduce a simple form of printing to children.

2. To use a familar object in a new way.

3. To develop a sense of rhythm through repetition.

(For Grades 4 through 6; adapted to Grades K through 3)

Lesson Two:

CATCH A FALLING LEAF

Leaf Printing

DO YOU THINK LEAVES JUST BELONG ON TREES? Oh, they're pretty there, of course, but they're pretty in other places, too. We'll use them to print a picture. So—catch a falling leaf and put in your picture—save it for a special day.

Have each child in your class bring in two or three leaves. Take a few minutes to talk about them. Perhaps they can identify the kinds of trees they came from. Notice their outlines—the sharp points of a pin oak; the smooth, rounded lines of a sassafras; the saw-tooth edge of an elm.

There is one way in which all leaves are the same. Have you noticed what it is? Look at the two sides of each leaf. The two sides aren't the same, are they? Each leaf has one smooth, rather shiny side, and one side that is much rougher and duller. The veins of the leaves stand out more on the back of the leaf—on the rougher side. The top of the leaf may look prettier, but the back of the leaf will help us to make a prettier picture.

While your class is gathered around you, prepare your printing materials: newspaper to cover the work area; a piece of 12″ x 18″ white or colored construction paper; a leaf or two; a little dab of tempera paint; a brush (paste brush, easel brush, watercolor brush—almost any kind of brush); another smaller piece of newspaper.

Now, let's see—I want to print this leaf so that it looks like this, the lovely lines of the veins as well as the outline. Should I put the paint on the smooth front of the leaf or the rough back of the leaf? Of course, I will put it on the back so that the rough part will print.

Spread a thin coat of paint over the vein side of the leaf. Now place it paint side down on your picture. Oh, you mustn't move it! That would smudge it, wouldn't it! I'll lay a little piece of newspaper over it so that I can rub it. What do you think is happening? Certainly, the paint is coming off the leaf onto my picture. Will the paint be smooth? No, not at all!

207

The leaf is rough, so the print it makes will be rough, too. See! There it is—not only the shape of the leaf but every tiny vein shows, too!

But one leaf doesn't make a picture, does it? So what should I do? Right! Repaint the vein side, lay it down on the picture again, cover it with a clean piece of newspaper, rub it gently—and there it is again! That's easy to do. Just keep on painting and printing until your whole picture is finished. Put the prints close together, but don't crowd them.

Cover desks with newspaper, pass out materials, choose one or two leaves. Oops, not too much paint! If there is too much paint on your leaf it will ooze out and spoil the shape—and the veins won't show, either. That's better—just a thin layer of paint.

Keep the prints close together. Each time you lay a leaf down to print it, turn it in a different direction. That will make a more interesting picture, won't it? It will help your eyes to move easily over the whole picture.

Walk about the room as the class continues to print. Add more paint to the palettes if it is needed. Give children more small pieces of newspaper to lay on their leaves before pressing them. (Each piece of newspaper can be used only once. If it were used again, wet paint on it from previous prints would spot the picture.)

That's a good print! It looks better when the print doesn't look solid, doesn't it? Remember, if you don't put on too much paint the print will look better.

When all your falling leaves have been caught and put into pictures, clean up the easy way. Let one person collect the brushes to be washed later. Have each child lay all the small pieces of newspaper and the palette on top of the newspaper that covers the desk. Just fold them with the leaves inside the newspaper so that they can easily be collected and thrown away. That's all there is to it—except, of course, admiring all those prints.

Make It Easy—for Yourself!

1. Cover all work areas with newspaper.
2. Use fresh leaves. Lay them between the pages of a magazine so that they will remain flat. Otherwise they will become crinkly as they dry.
3. Medium sized leaves will make more interesting arrangements than either tiny or extra large ones.
4. Use only a small amount of paint on the leaf. Too much paint tends to blot and spoil either the outline or vein design of the leaf.
5. Sometimes the first print is not satisfactory. Therefore, it is a good idea to print the leaf once on scrap paper before printing it on the picture.
6. A tiny amount of tempera paint on scrap paper makes a satisfactory palette that can be thrown away at the end of the lesson.
7. Cut newspapers into small pieces—about six inches square is a good size—to lay over the leaf while it is being rubbed to make the print. Each person should have several at the beginning of the lesson.

Variations

1. Use several kinds of leaves—or several colors—on the same print.
2. Print in a similar way with other familiar objects: scrap wood, bent wire, crumpled paper.
3. Cut a piece of fruit, or potato, or carrot in half and print with that. Or make simple cuts in the flat surface of the potato before printing.

Variations for Lower Grades

1. Print with simple objects like sponges, large erasers, the end of a pencil. Dip them into the paint instead of painting the color on.
2. Glue leaves to a background paper. (Use glue—not paste. The leaves will break and pull away from paste after it is dry.)

OBJECTIVES

1. To introduce three-dimensional art in the primary grades.

2. To increase the awareness of the beauty of trees by actually using parts of them.

3. To stimulate working and design-ing in the third dimension.

(For Grades K through 3)

Lesson Three:

WHEN IS A BRANCH NOT A BRANCH?

3-D Trees

WHEN IS A BRANCH NOT A BRANCH? WHEN IT'S A TREE.
Does this sound like one of your children's riddles? It's really quite
true. You can take ordinary branches or twigs and turn them into delightful
three-dimensional fantasy trees.

It's difficult to try to introduce three-dimensional sculpture to a young
child, but if you give him a point of reference, he soon learns that a three-
dimensional sculpture is a picture that stands up. You can easily get your
materials for the lesson. Take your class for a walk and look for small
twigs—or have the children bring in a few from home. The class will feel
very much a part of the lesson for they will donate part of the materials.

You now must turn these twigs into trees. What kind? How can this
be creative? Let's find out. If you have some clay, pieces of styrofoam, or
any material which can be punctured, use it for a base. Give each child a
small piece of clay, for example, and have him shape it into his own form.
He might want a simple square or rectangle, or a ball shape, or a pyramid.
When the base is finished, he starts constructing his "tree" with twigs. One
twig stuck in the clay already looks like a miniature tree. Although nature's
design is graceful, it certainly isn't very interesting or creative yet. Let's try
to turn it into a flower sculpture.

Take small squares of colored tissue paper and pinch the centers. Draw
them through your fingers to create beautiful little flowers. Apply a wad
of paste at the base of the tissue paper and attach it to the end of the twig.
Get the idea? We can design a beautiful flower sculpture by adding more
flowers and more twigs.

There are certain things to remember in a three-dimensional construction. Keep turning it so it looks good from every side. Have variety in the
height of your construction so that there will be tall places and short places.
Don't crowd too much into your sculpture or it will look messy. Remember
not to have everything sticking straight up—plan for a more graceful
arrangement of lines and spaces.

Our flowers can be made from several layers of tissue paper for a fuller bloom. Different colors may be overlapped for a rich looking flower.

Other materials may be used instead of tissue paper. Construction paper can be used for flat cut blossoms. Colored newsprint from the comics also make delightful flowers. Magazine illustrations lend themselves to shiny blossoms.

Other subjects can be utilized in our 3-D pictures. Underwater scenes, abstract cut paper shapes, geometric shapes, or just twigs painted and arranged in an exciting spidery construction can prove that our branch is not a branch.

Make It Easy—for Yourself!

1. Use only small twigs which can be supported from a simple base.
2. If styrofoam blocks or foam packing blocks are used, they may be painted first for a more finished look.
3. Twigs may be broken for more simple and direct sculpture.
4. If glue is available, it will support more weight on the branch for a longer period of time, but it will not stick right away. Apply the glue and let it get tacky before putting flowers on the twigs.
5. Use a small piece of manila or construction paper under the clay to absorb the oils.
6. Cover the desk with newspaper to protect the surface if you use glue.

Variations

1. Make the same kind of clay base, but make your construction from thin applicator sticks. These can be broken for different lengths and painted for a brighter finish. The sculpture can be done with just sticks stuck into the base from all sides to resemble a star burst. This can also be done with toothpicks for a smaller construction.
2. Use either sticks or twigs to make a holiday construction. Decorated Easter eggs, valentine hearts, Christmas motifs, and Thanksgiving foods are only a few holiday ideas for sculpture.

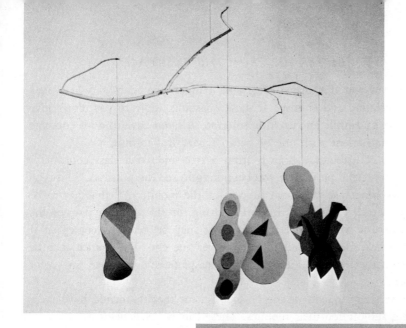

O B J E C T I V E S

1. To introduce the art of making mobiles.

2. To stimulate an interest in three-dimensional work.

3. To teach design and balance by making a mobile structure.

4. To see how the beauty of nature may be used in an art object.

(For Grades 5 and 6)

Lesson Four:

NATURE'S BEAUTIFUL FORMS

Branch Mobiles

ARE YOU ONE OF THOSE PEOPLE WHO HAVE always wanted to make dramatic mobiles in your classroom? Have you been intimidated because of the seemingly complex problems of constructing one? Are you dissatisfied with coat hanger-type mobiles which may look uninteresting and clumsy? If these questions apply to you, don't give up, for there's a simple and exciting solution. All you have to do is combine a little human talent with one of nature's beautiful forms.

Nature contributes a branch from a tree and your class contributes its ability to cut and paste. Are you beginning to see the possibilities? Imagine the tree branch as the main support of the mobile. All that has to be done is to attach a piece of thin wire, string, or thread on a part of the branch where it will balance it. This point may be near the center or, if the branch has a lot of smaller parts, nearer one end. The branch may be left in its natural state or it may be either painted or sprayed any color you desire.

Before your students decide on a finish for their branches, have them think of a subject for their mobiles. These can be as general as freeform shapes or as specific as an underwater scene, ballet, horses, or anything they'd enjoy making from cut paper. When the subject has been selected, each child works out his own designs by cutting out figures from a double piece of construction paper, getting two identical shapes. Place the end of a piece of string or thread in the middle of the shape, apply paste around the edges, and top it with its twin shape. The string is now secured between the two cut shapes.

If the student decides to paint his branch, this should be done before the shapes are cut, so that the branch will be dry when it is time to suspend the cut shapes from it. Have each child find the balancing point on his branch and tie a piece of string to it. The loose end of the string can be taped to the edge of the desk to test the balance of the branch. One by one each cut shape is tied onto the branch first at one end, then the other in order to maintain the original balance. Different lengths of string should be used for a more interesting and graceful mobile. Each shape should be able to move and spin without hitting another.

When the mobiles are finished, they should be hung from a high place so that they can move and dance and delight everyone. It's simple to create these charming friends when you combine talent with nature's beautiful forms.

Make It Easy—for Yourself!

1. Have each child select his own branch and bring it to school. Suggest that they look for dead branches found on the ground.
2. Limit the size of the branch for the first lesson. Don't have a child try to manage too large a branch.

3. Have a discussion about different ideas for subject matter. Choose one subject and see how many things can be cut out to fit that subject.
4. Use paste, not glue, and apply it freely. When the paste dries it becomes stiff and helps support the shapes.
5. Show the class some examples of balance by demonstrating how a small shape near the end can balance a large shape nearer the center.

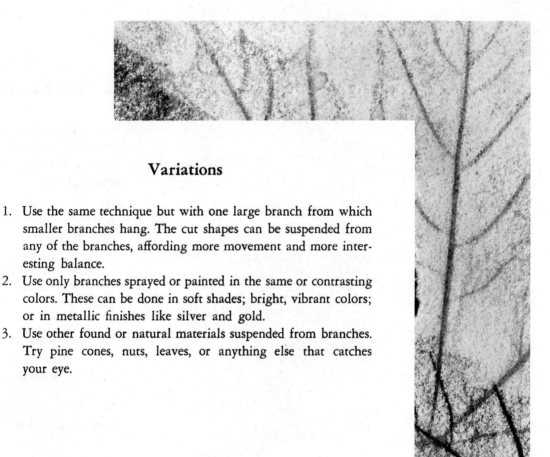

Variations

1. Use the same technique but with one large branch from which smaller branches hang. The cut shapes can be suspended from any of the branches, affording more movement and more interesting balance.
2. Use only branches sprayed or painted in the same or contrasting colors. These can be done in soft shades; bright, vibrant colors; or in metallic finishes like silver and gold.
3. Use other found or natural materials suspended from branches. Try pine cones, nuts, leaves, or anything else that catches your eye.

OBJECTIVES

1. To learn to observe closely and to see the details that are often overlooked.

2. To learn to draw things as they appear.

3. To learn to create a feeling or mood in a picture.

4. To use a natural material as a novelty within a picture.

5. To learn to overlap parts of a picture.

6. To learn that all objects in a picture need to be on a base (the ground).

(For Grades 1 through 6)

Lesson Five:

TREES FROM
TINY BRANCHES GROW

Branches in Realistic Pictures

YOU KNOW THAT "TREES FROM tiny acorns grow"—but that takes too long! Let's make a picture in which trees from tiny branches grow.

It's a dreary winter day. You'd like an appropriate art lesson—but on a day like this? Of course. Let's plan one that's especially for a cold, dull winter day.

Do things look the same in winter as they do in summer? Does a landscape look the same? No, of course not! That's right, there may be snow on the ground. And then the ground looks white instead of being mostly green grass the way it is in the summer. Even if there isn't any snow, the grass looks different in the winter, doesn't it? The green is duller—even has lots of brown in it. The colors are different in winter than in summer, aren't they? They are . . . right, they are duller.

Look out the window. Notice the color of the ground—the color of the sky. They aren't nearly as bright as they were last summer. There's another reason, too, why things aren't as gay and bright as in the summer. Something is missing. Flowers! Of course! In the summer there will be roses, and geraniums, and morning glories, and asters—all kinds of flowers. And flowers are bright—reds, blues, yellows—all kinds of colors. So when there aren't any flowers in blossom, everything looks duller and grayer.

When you make a winter picture, there's another way you will make it look different from a summer picture. Would you expect to see more people outdoors in winter or in summer? Surely—more people would be outside in summer—mowing the lawn, working in the garden, playing on the swings. But in the winter it is too cold to stay outside long, so unless they have to go out—or maybe make a snowman—people like to stay in their warm houses.

And how about the trees? They are very different in winter than in summer, aren't they? Talk about summer trees—the way the branches spread out and up, the masses of green leaves that cover them. But look at them now. There aren't any green leaves, are there? All you see are bare branches—lots of them. So in your winter picture there will be trees without any leaves on them. You will see branches, branches, branches—but no leaves.

There is one kind of tree, though, that looks the same in winter as it does in summer. That's right. It is called an evergreen tree because the needles on it stay green all winter.

When your pictures are all finished—when every bit of the paper has been covered with crayon—you may put some *real* trees in your pictures. Show them the evergreen branches and the bare twigs. See, they can be glued right on your paper. It will be like planting real trees. You can put them in the front yard of one of your houses—or mix them in with a clump of trees you have drawn in your picture. Pictures with real things in them are very special!

Now let's begin our winter pictures—dull colors with perhaps snow on the ground; trees without leaves on them; no flowers; few if any people in them.

Have crayons that have a good assortment of colors so that there will be a variety of dull and dark colors to choose from. Talk about which ones look like winter colors. Would you use the bright green? No, the dark green would be better. Or perhaps you have a yellow green. You wouldn't use the bright red, either, would you? Dark red would be fine—or pink. Certainly, pink is red—just another way of saying light red. Yes, brown and black and gray would be fine, too.

As the children begin to draw their pictures, remind them of the things that will help to make them winter pictures instead of summer pictures. After the pictures have a house or two in them, take a look outdoors again. Can you see any house that is partly in back of another house? Point out a house or other building that is partly covered by another one. Notice trees that are partly in front of or in back of something else. You could do that, too, couldn't you?

Encourage children to add details to their pictures. What is usually on top of the roof of a house? Yes—a chimney! Yes, you're right, too— a television aerial! That looks much more like a house. Can you think of anything you might see at the windows? What might be in the street in front of the house? What else might be in the yard?

Usually young children will start their pictures by putting in a line for the ground and then adding objects on top of the line. When you encouraged them to put in other things that are farther back, they probably just put them up higher on the paper—off the ground. Go to the blackboard and quickly sketch a picture with several houses or other objects that are up in the air.

Ask the class what is wrong with your picture. Probably someone will tell you that a house is up in the air. If they don't see that right away, point out the ground and the house that is on it. This will help them to see what is wrong. So make the ground come all the way up to whatever is highest in your picture—like that. Now everything is on the ground, isn't it?

Let each child choose a real tree or two. When all the crayon work has been finished, he may find a good place to plant his tree. Spread the glue along each branch before holding them tightly against the paper. There—a winter picture with real trees—trees that grew from tiny branches!

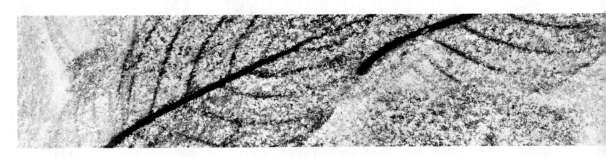

Make It Easy—for Yourself!

1. Urge the children to press hard on their crayons in some parts of their pictures. Make some parts of the pictures stronger and more important than other parts.
2. Cut off branches about six to ten inches long. If you keep them between the pages of a magazine they will flatten slightly and be easier to glue to the pictures.
3. Use glue to hold the "real" trees to the pictures. Paste is not strong enough and will pull off. It takes time for the glue to begin to dry and take hold, so hold the branches firmly against the paper for a minute or two. (Keep glue off furniture.)
4. The needles on the evergreen branches will eventually dry and fall off, but those that have been glued will remain on the paper. Even if they all come off it is no problem—they just become regular winter trees!

Variation

Make a forest of "real" trees. Color (with crayon or paint) only the ground and sky.

OBJECTIVES

1. To learn to observe
   more closely—to learn
   to see the things we
   usually merely look at.

2. To be more aware of
   the natural beauty
   around us.

3. To be aware of line as
   an important part of
   design.

4. To introduce the idea
   of background space
   as an important part
   of the picture.

(For Grades 3 through 6)

Lesson Six:

ONLY A SHADOW

Drawing Trees

HAVE YOU EVER LOOKED DOWN—AND THERE AT your feet found an intricate design? It was only a shadow, but for an instant you felt as though you were high in a tree among delicately forking branches.

Some warm, sunny day in early spring or late fall when you'd much rather be outdoors than in a classroom, you can be in both places. Take your class outdoors for an art lesson. Make sure it is the time of year when there are no leaves on the trees. This will be a magic art lesson. Give each child a piece of charcoal and a sheet of 12" x 18" white drawing paper.

When you are outside, look *down* to find a tree—just the shadow, that is. Look around for a while until you think you have found just the right spot. Lay your paper on the ground. See, you have a picture already. But move it a bit. Now it looks different, doesn't it?

Move your paper back and forth. Which way do you like it best? Do you like it with all tiny, veinlike lines—or do you like it better when there are different thicknesses to the lines? Yes, it does look better with more variety to the size of the branches. Continue to change the position of the paper: slant it a little this way or that; move it so there is an interesting direction to the lines; move it again until the shapes of the background are interesting, some large, some small. Change it until you are pleased with your design.

There, that's just the way I want my picture to look. There's just one trouble—it is only a shadow! What will happen if I pick up my paper? Of course—the whole picture will disappear. But that isn't much of a problem for we can draw the shadow that is on the paper. The lines for us are already there, so all we have to do is fill them in with charcoal.

As you talk, begin to draw the lines that are on your paper. Sketch them quickly, drawing in each tiny variation of line. Don't leave out any-thing—it is the picture exactly as the shadow is making it that looks good.

221

Draw only one small section of the picture. That's enough to show how to do it. Still, there is one thing wrong with that part of the picture. Hold your hand above your picture so that its shadow covers part of what you have already drawn. What's the matter with it—how is it different from the shadow "drawing"? The shadow is . . . ? Right, the shadow is solid and the charcoal drawing is only an outline. That doesn't look as good, does it? So use your charcoal to fill in the space between the lines so that it looks just like the picture made by the shadow.

By this time each person will be anxious to find his own shadow picture. Encourage each child to experiment before he makes a final selection. Move about the class offering suggestions where they are needed and complimenting those who have made a pleasing selection.

When a few children have completed their drawings, get the group together. There is one more thing you can do to make your pictures look even better. A shadow looks smooth—almost soft, but the charcoal seems rough and hard. Wrap a piece of face tissue around your index finger and carefully blend the lines of the charcoal. Of course, you can do that only on the large areas. The small areas don't need it—and it would probably spoil the edges to even try it. Notice how sharp and clean-cut the edges of the shadow are. Keep yours the same way.

Success will be assured for each child, and you will want to display each person's work. They were only shadows, but now they are delicately designed pictures that you will be proud to show.

Make It Easy—for Yourself!

1. Pick a clear day when the sun casts crisp, definite shadows.
2. If the paper is taped to a "drawing board" it will be easier to handle. Satisfactory drawing boards may be made from a piece of cardboard a little larger than the paper to be used. A piece of masking tape at each corner will hold it in place during the drawing.
3. Use the charcoal sparingly when filling in areas so as not to leave unused charcoal on the paper.
4. Smooth only the large areas and do not get too close to the edges of them. Keep the edges sharp.
5. If the finished pictures are to be displayed where someone may rub against them, spray them lightly with fixative. Hair spray makes an excellent fixative substitute if none of the regular aerosol type is available.

Variations

1. Use other materials—one color of crayon or paint—for a similar type of picture.
2. Find other interesting shadows and make pictures of them.
3. Draw trees from observation. Notice the variety of thicknesses of different parts: trunk, limbs, branches, twigs. Notice how they grow out of each other, how they cross over each other.

OBJECTIVES

1. To use an ordinary "found" object to make a useful article.

2. To use paint in a free and accidental way.

(For Grades K through 4; adapted to Grades 5 and 6)

Lesson Seven:

NO ROLLING STONE

Paperweights from Stones

WHO WANTS A STONE TO GATHER
moss! Not us, but just the same be sure the stones you gather are flat. For
a stone that has one flat side will make a wonderful paperweight—or if
it's too big for that, you might use it for a doorstop. So, no rolling stones.

Have the children look around their backyards, or on their way to
school—anywhere at all for a stone that is reasonably smooth and flat
on one side. It may be paperweight size—small enough to fit nicely into
your hand—or if it is too large for that, it may be heavy enough for a
practical doorstop.

Once you have just the right stones, the rest is easy. Simply have a
variety of colors of tempera paint. Let each child take a spoonful of paint
and pour it over the stone. See how it drips over the rounding sides and
then drops off onto the newspaper that is covering the desk. Makes pretty
colored lines, doesn't it? Well, let's try it again, perhaps with another color.

Plan the colors you want your paperweight to be—perhaps just a
couple, perhaps four or five. If you want the colors to blend together, add
another color while the preceding one is still wet. If you want each color
to be distinct, wait for each one to dry before adding the next one. You may
cover the whole stone with paint or leave some of the natural color still
showing. But whichever you do, it will be the gayest stone you have ever
seen.

After the paint has dried, give the stone two coats of varnish. This
will give it a protective finish as well as a shiny one. When the varnish
is thoroughly dry, glue a piece of felt or heavy cloth to the flat, bottom
part of the stone. This will protect the finish of whatever surface the
paperweight (or doorstop) is used on. It won't gather moss—but it won't
be a rolling stone either.

225

Make It Easy—for Yourself!

1. Cover all work areas with newspaper.
2. Let several children work together, sharing painting and varnishing materials.
3. Enamel paint may be used in place of tempera paint. In that case it will not be necessary to varnish the stone. However, enamel paint takes longer to dry.
4. Allow at least a day between coats of varnish so that the first one will be thoroughly dry.
5. Use turpentine to clean the brushes that were used to apply the varnish (or enamel paint if that was used).

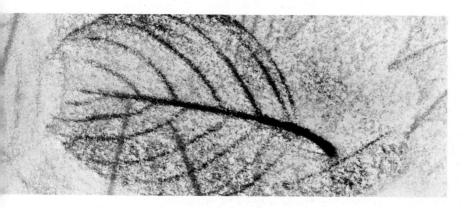

Variation

Find rocks that have interesting natural colors or markings. Apply only varnish to preserve their natural beauty while at the same time giving them a glossy finish.

Variation for Higher Grades

Glue groups of small stones together for a paperweight. (Marbles may be used in place of small stones.) Use plenty of a quick drying glue so they will stay together. If you glue the bottom layer to a piece of cardboard, it will help to hold them in place and make it easier to add other layers of stones.

OBJECTIVES

1. To create a sculptured form.

2. To capitalize on a natural and familiar interest.

3. To learn about the properties of a new material and how to work with it.

4. To have the experience of working directly in a pliable media.

(For Grades 3 through 6)

Lesson Eight:

JUST A GRAIN OF SAND— WELL, SEVERAL!

Sandcasting

YOU'VE PLAYED IN THE SAND AT THE SEASHORE, haven't you? You probably made castles and mountains and all kinds of things in the damp sand. But when the tide came in—one wave, and they were all washed away. We won't need the whole beachful of sand, just a grain of it—well, several! And we'll make those wonderful things last forever!

You'll need a few other common materials, too, before beginning your sandcasting. So have ready plaster of Paris, a pail or other container to mix the plaster in, some water, and some small boxes or plastic containers to hold the damp sand.

It will be better to work outdoors to do away with any clean-up in the room. Give each child a small container of some kind—a cardboard box, a deep papier-mâché container (the kind fruit sometimes comes in), a plastic ice cream container—almost anything that will hold an inch or so of damp sand. Be sure the sand is just damp enough to hold a shape but not wet enough to accumulate extra water.

Let's just play in it for a while. Does it remind you of last summer when you were at the beach? See how you can dig the sand out of some areas and pile it in other places. You can make it smooth or leave it rough, can't you?

While the children continue to "play" in the sand, mix a container of plaster of Paris. Pour in a quantity of water equal to the amount of plaster you want. Slowly pour the plaster of Paris into it, continuing to stir the mixture. You will probably be surprised by how much plaster you need. Continue to add more until it begins to be a little bit creamy. There may be a slight warmth to it caused by the chemical reaction taking place.

When the mixture is completely smooth and slightly creamy, it is ready for use. Let each child have a paper cupful of plaster of Paris (he will need to return for a second or third cupful). Be sure you pour it carefully over your sand so that it won't change the shapes you have created. Pour in plaster until you think the whole thing is covered with at least a half inch of the liquid.

There—now we'll wait until it has become firm.

In the meantime let's clean up. And in this case it is an important part of our work. *Don't let one bit of plaster get into the sink!* If you used a throw-away container for mixing the plaster, do just that—throw it away. No plaster from that will get into the sink! Collect the paper cups and throw them away. No plaster from them will get into the sink! Have a pail of water and a supply of paper towels. Anyone who has plaster on his hands—including you who mixed it—must rinse his hands in the pail. That water can then be emptied into the schoolyard. No plaster from that will get into the sink!

What do you suppose has been happening to our sandcastings while we have been cleaning up? Surely—the plaster has begun to get firm and hard. What will it look like when it is removed from the sand? Yes, there will be sand stuck to it. In fact we will have to push the damp sand off our casting. We will even have to rinse it off in water—or pour some water over it. Even then a little sand will be stuck into the plaster, but that will give it an interesting texture and make it look good.

Do you think the plaster will be the same shape as the sand was? Well—not quite. In fact, it will be just the opposite. That's right! Where there was a low spot in the sand the plaster went in and filled it. So now it will be like a hill on the plaster. Yes, and where there was a hill on the sand there will be a low spot on the plaster.

If you didn't get enough plaster in the water, don't worry about it.

The heavier plaster will sink to the bottom of your casting and the extra water will form on the surface. Plaster of Paris hardens even under water (that's the reason *none* must get into the sink!). So when it is firm all you will have to do is pour off the extra water. See, it really is easy!

Now for unveiling our masterpieces. If your sandcasting is in a metal or plastic container, stretch one hand out over the surface of your sand-casting so that as much of the surface is covered by your hand as is possible. Now tip the whole thing over on your hand. It may drop out easily. If it doesn't, hit the bottom of the container firmly with your other hand. Out will come your casting—and sand, too—so hold it over newspaper to catch the extra sand. You can use that over again, you know. If your sandcasting is in a cardboard box, tear off the sides of the box and remove the plaster. Use your fingers to push off as much sand as possible.

Let's clean it up a bit. How will we do that? Just rinse it in a pail of water. Out it comes with just enough sand still stuck to it to give it a pleasing texture. It will take a while for it to dry thoroughly. In the meantime, treat it gently so as not to break it. Horrors—wouldn't that be awful!

Make It Easy—for Yourself!

1. Work outside if possible. If sand or water or plaster gets on the ground no harm is done—in the classroom it might become a considerable problem.
2. Have all of your materials organized before the beginning of the lesson: pail of water for rinsing hands; container of water for mixing plaster; extra water for mixing another batch of plaster if it is needed; paper towels; paper cups; containers for sandcasting; damp sand; plaster of Paris; flat stick to stir the plaster.
3. Press the sand firmly together to form the mold.
4. A few drops of vinegar added to the water will slow the setting process of the plaster of Paris. This is an advantage when you are working with a number of people at one time. If the plaster of Paris begins to harden before it is poured over the sand, there is nothing you can do with it. Throw it away and begin over again. More water will not thin it if it has begun to set.
5. Don't let any plaster get into the sink! Plaster will set—become hard—even in the middle of a pool of water. That is why more water will not thin or dilute it once it has begun to set. You may want to cover over the sink with a piece of cardboard or newspaper as a reminder not to wash hands or containers there.

6. Don't be alarmed if a layer of water forms on the surface of your sandcasting. There just wasn't enough plaster of Paris in the mixture, but what was there has sunk to the bottom and will harden. So when the plaster is firm, tip the container and pour off the extra water—outside, that is—not in the sink!

7. Explain the whole process in the beginning so that the class knows what to expect and the reason why they are doing certain things—and the precautions that are being taken. Once the plaster is ready to use there will be no time for explanations—it must be used immediately.

8. Allow plenty of drying time before removing the plaster casting. If the plaster is wet, it may break as it is removed. It will be necessary to take a second lesson to remove the casts.

9. If you can arrange it, work with only half of your class at one time. The next day let the other half of the class make their sandcastings. You will find it easier to prepare the plaster of Paris for the smaller group—and the results will be better.

10. You may add some tempera paint to the water before mixing the plaster of Paris, if you want to color it.

Variations

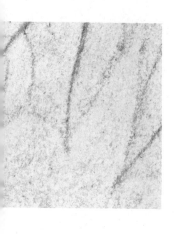

1. Give each child a small pile of damp sand on top of wax paper or aluminum foil. Dig a shape in the sand and pour plaster of Paris into it. The surrounding sand forms the mold so that a container is unnecessary.

2. Prepare a form or base with non-hardening clay instead of damp sand. You will not even need a box to hold it if you build up the sides with clay. (Keep it thick.) Press and mold the clay the same as you would the sand. Pour in plaster of Paris and allow to harden. Remove from the clay form.

3. Put a smooth layer of non-hardening clay (about an inch thick) in the bottom of a box or other container. Use one or more objects (nail heads, blunt ends of pencils, ends of rulers, dowels) to press into the clay. Press the objects in and out of the clay over and over again to create an allover repeat pattern in the clay base. Pour plaster of Paris into the container until it is almost an inch thick. Allow to dry and remove. The plaster of Paris will have penetrated all the holes created in the repeat pattern.

OBJECTIVES

1. To introduce bas-relief through a new technique.

2. To increase an awareness of form and texture.

3. To use a familiar material in an unusual way.

(For Grades 4 through 6)

Lesson Nine:

PAINT WITH SAND!

Bas-Relief Pictures

YOU'VE PAINTED WITH PAINT—HOW ABOUT painting with sand? Yes, sand—ordinary, fine-grained beach sand. You can create beautiful sculpture-like pictures that will astound everyone.

Use a sturdy piece of cardboard and have each child sketch a simple picture. It can be about any subject but it should contain one large object which will become raised from the background. After he has finished his simplified drawing, the artist is now ready to apply the sand.

He needs a small container of water, a brush, liquid white glue, and, of course, some sand. The sand may be handed out in paper plates, shoe boxes, or any kind of containers.

First, care should be taken by the student to wet his brush thoroughly with water. When it is soaked through, he shakes off any excess liquid, and dips it into the glue. He then paints a small area of the main object of his

picture, coating it evenly with the glue. Quickly he sprinkles sand on the wet glue, making sure all the glue is covered. Gently he shakes the excess sand back into its container, and continues glueing and sanding.

His main object is now a flat silhouette of sand. The details of the original drawing must now be brought back by more layers of sand. Glue is painted on carefully where a raised surface is desired, then the surface is sprinkled, and finally the excess sand is shaken off. As more layers are applied the details are brought out in relief as high as desired.

When the relief is finished, with many layers, the background can be sanded, painted, or even covered with cut paper. It's up to the artist, but it would not be good to have it too thick or it would detract from the bas-relief.

When these bas-reliefs are dry they give the effect of carved stone, and you will be pleased with the compliments and the amazed looks when you tell how they were painted with sand.

Make It Easy—for Yourself!

1. Cover all desks or tables with newspaper to avoid marring the surfaces.
2. Use a cup or scoop to distribute the sand into the individual con-containers.
3. Make sure brushes are soaked with water before dipping them into the glue. Wet them occasionally during the lesson, and wash them with mild soap and warm water immediately after they have been used.
4. Have a sink or basin filled with warm soapy water in which to put the brushes if they can't be washed quickly. Don't let the glue dry on them.
5. Have the class keep their subject matter simple. Use a small piece of cardboard for the first trial.
6. If small individual bottles of glue are used, a small amount may be squeezed out of the bottle, then spread with the wet brush.

Variations

1. When the bas-relief picture is finished, paint over it with tempera. This can be done with one color to maintain a sculptured look, or in a few colors as in a regularly painted picture.
2. If other sand-like material is available—such as marble dust or rock dust—use the same technique. Test the material before using it.

OBJECTIVES

1. To make a useful and decorative three-dimensional design.

2. To learn to create rhythmical lines in a three-dimensional form.

3. To have the experience of selecting and arranging found materials to create a pleasing three-dimensional design.

4. To experience the satisfaction of creating something of value to contribute to the home.

5. To learn to see the beauty of natural materials.

(For Grades 4 through 6)

Lesson Ten:

AND IT'S FREE!

Dried Table Decorations

HAVE YOU EVER BEEN TEMPTED TO buy one of those elaborate—and expensive—artificial flower arrangements? Well, don't! You can make one you'll like even better—and it's free, too!

The first early days of fall are a warning that winter is on its way.

233

So let's prepare for it by gathering materials for our own special table decorations that will last throughout the winter months. The variety of materials you can find is almost endless: cattails, empty milkweed, pampas grass, pine cones, acorns, rose hips, bayberries, bittersweet. Every part of the country has its own special kinds of trees which develop interesting seed pods. Some of them even have leaves that can be dried on the stem without becoming brittle and falling off.

You will need only two other materials in addition to the dried materials—non-hardening clay and a piece of scrap wood for the base of each arrangement.

When the day to make the decorations arrives, it will be an exciting time. Let each child spread his assortment of treasures on his work area. Talk about them for a few minutes. Point out a tall material that will make a good beginning for an arrangement. Maybe that one is even too tall! It might be top-heavy and make your arrangement tip over. So you may want to break off the steam just a little bit. Those small pine cones will be good to fill in at the bottom, won't they? They could help to cover some of the clay so that the base of your table decoration would be interesting, too.

But enough just looking! Let's begin to arrange all these things into lovely three-dimensional designs. Give each person a small amount of non-hardening clay—enough to make a little mound on the wood which will be the base of the design. Squeeze the clay enough to slightly soften it. Then press it into a high mound on the base. Remember, it is to hold all the stems of your arrangement, so it must be in a pile in order to be strong enough.

Now let's begin by sticking something tall into that pile of clay. If it's too tall and feels wobbly, just break off the bottom of the stem to make it a little shorter. There—that's a good beginning!

Continue adding parts to the arrangement. If you were arranging these things in a vase, they would all start from about the same place, wouldn't they? So do the same thing now. Make all the stems start from about the same place. They will look better that way. But they won't all go straight up, will they? Some of them may lean more to one side to make a pleasing line arrangement.

As you walk about the room, compliment a child on his good beginning or the fine choice of materials he has. Suggest a material to fill in an empty area or show how a slight change will add a new and interesting line. Ask a question—or answer one. Do you need something at the bottom of the design to help cover the clay? Certainly you may share your materails!

Turn your arrangement in all directions. Does it look good from every side? If it does, you are finished. It's a surprise, isn't it, that you could find such lovely things! Everyone will be surprised, too, that you made such beautiful arrangements. They look so expensive, but we know they are free.

Make It Easy—for Yourself!

1. Have each child bring his dry materials to school in a large paper bag that has his name on it. This will make it easy to store the materials until you are ready to use them.
2. Cover each area with a large sheet of newspaper. This will hold all the discarded materials and make it easy to clean up at the end of the lesson. Just roll all the scraps inside the paper and discard the whole thing.
3. If milkweed is brought in, have the children empty the pods of all fly-away seeds in the fields where they find them.
4. Have a sharing area where extra materials may be placed and used by other children.
5. Use any kind of wood for the base: an irregularly shaped piece of scrap lumber, driftwood, a large piece of bark. An unusual base will help create an interesting arrangement.
6. Don't flatten the clay. Leave it in a high mound. This will give it strength to hold the stems. Press the edges against the wood to hold the clay firmly in place.
7. Gradually add shorter and shorter things to the arrangement so that as much of the clay as possible will be hidden.

Variations

1. If desired, spray the arrangement with gold or silver.
2. Make a two-dimensional arrangement of pressed and dried materials. Collect grasses, ferns, weeds, leaves. Place them between pages of a magazine until they are dry and flat. Arrange them on a piece of wax paper, cover with another piece of wax paper. Iron with a medium hot iron. This will seal the dry materials between the layers of wax paper and create an interesting, transparent design.

INDEX

Please remember that this is a library book,
and that it belongs only temporarily to each
person who uses it. Be considerate. Do
not write in this, or any, library book.